Hanging In

Strategies for Teaching the
Students Who Challenge Us Most

■ ■ ■

Jeffrey
BENSON

Hanging In

Strategies for Teaching the
Students Who Challenge Us Most

Alexandria, Virginia USA

1703 N. Beauregard St. • Alexandria, VA 22311-1714 USA
Phone: 800-933-2723 or 703-578-9600 • Fax: 703-575-5400
Website: www.ascd.org • E-mail: member@ascd.org
Author guidelines: www.ascd.org/write

Gene R. Carter, *Executive Director;* Richard Papale, *Publisher;* Stefani Roth, *Acquisitions Editor;* Julie Houtz, *Director, Book Editing & Production;* Ernesto Yermoli, *Editor;* Thomas Lyttle, *Graphic Designer;* Mike Kalyan, *Production Manager;* Keith Demmons, *Desktop Publishing Specialist*

All web links in this book are correct as of the publication date below but may have become inactive or otherwise modified since that time. If you notice a deactivated or changed link, please e-mail books@ascd.org with the words "Link Update" in the subject line. In your message, please specify the web link, the book title, and the page number on which the link appears.

ASCD Member Book No. FY14- 4A (January 2014, PSI+). ASCD Member Books mail to Premium (P), Select (S), and Institutional Plus (I+) members on this schedule: Jan, PSI+; Feb, P; Apr, PSI+; May P; Jul, PSI+; Aug, P; Sep, PSI+; Nov, PSI+; Dec, P. For up-to-date details on membership, see www.ascd.org/membership.

PAPERBACK ISBN: 978-1-4166-1755-6   ASCD product #114013
Also available as an e-book (see Books in Print for the ISBNs).

Quantity discounts: 10–49 copies, 10%; 50+ copies, 15%; for 1,000 or more copies, call 800-933-2723, ext. 5634, or 703-575-5634. For desk copies: www.ascd.org/deskcopy.

Library of Congress Cataloging-in-Publication Data

Benson, Jeffrey.
  Hanging in : strategies for teaching the students who challenge us most / Jeffrey Benson.
      pages cm
  Includes bibliographical references and index.
  ISBN 978-1-4166-1755-6 (pbk. : alk. paper) 1. Problem children–Education–United States. 2. Learning disabled children–Education–United States. I. Title.
  LC4802.B46 2014
  371.9–dc23
                              2013038030

23 22 21 20 19 18 17 16 15 14   1 2 3 4 5 6 7 8 9 10 11 12

Hanging In

Strategies for Teaching the
Students Who Challenge Us Most

■ ■ ■

Introduction

I was chairing an hour-long meeting with school administrators, teachers, therapists, and support staff. The group had convened to deal with a single issue: how Dean, a volatile 4th grader, could more successfully transition from class to class. Dean insisted on being first in line, argued over every expectation, and swore at staff as he quickly lost his temper. He was exhausting his teachers, classmates, and everyone who was called in to de-escalate him and then assess his readiness for rejoining his class. We hypothesized what triggered Dean's reactions. We reviewed his complex family history, his ability to cognitively understand directions, and his ability to physically manage the passage from one room to another. We reviewed what staff had been saying to him, what rewards and punishments had been tried (all so far without lasting success), what the quality of his relationships was with peers and school staff, and what our overlapping goals were for Dean and the school. By the end of the hour, we had synthesized our perspectives and developed a plan (the focus of Chapter 2 in this book). At that point, the principal turned to me and said, "That should do the trick." I sighed and responded, "There are no tricks."

There are no tricks to working with our most challenging students. If there were simple solutions to support their growth, the students wouldn't be challenging. The professionals most responsible for dealing with these students—among many and most often, special education teachers, social workers, occupational therapists—do not have a secret cache of techniques. These professionals have received training in identifying disabilities and employing common interventions, but our most challenging students confound common solutions. These students crisscross categories of disabilities, challenging us to develop new and complex interventions, in combinations we have never tried before.

In examining the effect solely of trauma on students, Cole and colleagues (2005, p. 4) identify a long list of potential problems: decreased concentration, fragmented memory, poor organization, language deficits, perfectionism, depression, anxiety, and self-destructive behavior. It is reasonable to add to this list excessive absences, uneven skill development, and deficits in content knowledge. Now add a learning disability and all its possible presentations. There are no textbook cases that point to absolute interventions for students with such layered lists of issues. Each child is truly unique, and we can't "fix them" immediately.

The challenge for the staff is to hang in. Students like Dean can shed maladaptive behaviors for better ones, but not overnight. These students remind us that humans don't change as much as grow. We grow through support, useful feedback, trust, safety, and time. There is no guarantee that any intervention will work, and there are no guarantees that growth will happen within a given period of time. Hattie (2009), in summarizing his extensive studies on student learning, writes:

> Learning is spontaneous, individualistic, and often earned through effort. It is a timeworn, slow, gradual, fits-and-starts kind of process, which can have a flow of its own, but requires passion, patience, and attention to detail. (p. 2)

With no reliably predictable timetable for success, these students try our patience, arouse our emotions, and often bruise our professional pride as teachers, problem solvers, and caretakers. Dean's difficulty transitioning between classes triggered anger in some staff. For others he provoked sadness—"When Dean is like that, I'd rather be any other person in the world than that little guy." For many, Dean brought up feelings of incompetence and despair. They were professional helpers, and Dean would not let them help; his failure became their failure. We have been schooling children for many centuries, yet a 10-year-old was baffling the experts. Mary Haywood Metz (1993) notes that students "can confirm or destroy" a teacher's "pride in craft." She explains the students' power: "Because teachers' work consists of affecting their students, they are dependent on their students both for the actual success of their work and evidence of that success" (p. 130).

We are in the infancy of understanding what works for every child, at the beginning stage of identifying practices that can cut across community, cultural, and personal contexts. Dean has no researched cohort—in his case, an upbringing in poverty with a single mother, a disabled older sibling, attention deficit disorder (ADD), advanced language skills, and the experience of having switched schools three times. His case is unique. So we hang in, take actions, reflect on progress, recalibrate, take more actions, collect our stories, and recalibrate again. We hang in. We may have to hang in through as many as 100 repetitions for a student to grow into new skills and for us to learn what works (Benson, 2012).

Everyone who hung in with Dean learned a lot, and we are all better at what we do because of that work. A challenging student provides one of the best means of reaching mastery in our field—but only when teachers themselves get support and safety, and when they are not dealing with many such students in isolation. Hanging in with challenging students can be so meaningful and reveal to us the richness and novelty of human relationships. What we experience in schools reinforces our uniquely human capacities to accommodate, synthesize, learn, and grow.

Storytelling

As I chaired the meeting about Dean, I knew we could not pull a manual off a shelf to find step-by-step directions to solve his problems. Instead, I combed through my years of teaching experience, looking for a student and set of conditions that resembled, in some key components, what was happening with Dean. I knew I would not find an exact match with his environment, *and* with his cognitive abilities, *and* with his chaotic life, *and* with his age. But I did find a promising story.

I said to the team, "I once worked with a student named Charlie, and we. . . ." With my storytelling, I was inviting the others to find similarities and differences, or as we might say in a basic English class, to compare and contrast the setting, the characters, and the primary conflict in Dean's story with the one I was telling about Charlie. The story about Charlie—who was 10 years older and of a different race, economic class, and cognitive ability—did spark our creative solutions for Dean. Buried within all those differences were important, but not so obvious, parallels. My expertise, born of experience and theory, was in identifying the parallels, the most salient aspects of one context with another. The group's collective wisdom pulled the relevant elements from Charlie's story into a useful intervention for Dean.

What I offer in this book are stories of hanging in, the practice-based evidence from working with our most challenging students, and the wisdom I have gleaned from each. Many of my experiences come from working in special education settings. The intimacy of small classes (8 students with one teacher) and of small schools (100 students) provides the opportunity to drill deeply into the complex layers of social, emotional, cognitive, cultural, economic, and environmental factors that make each student who he or she is. There is never one thing that defines a challenging student, never one cause, never one life event, never one disability. As noted above, if it were one thing, the solutions would be simple. One of my own teachers confronted me with this important and demanding advice: "Keep the complexity as long as you can." My stories invite you to hang in with the complexities of our challenging students and to take action with no guarantees of immediately observable success. The only guarantee is more evidence that you can use with the next challenging student—because I can guarantee you, there will be another one who challenges your capacity to hang in.

With that evidence, we must work together along the path from stories to informed practice. Just as two people can have a different interpretation of the motives of Rick Blaine, Humphrey Bogart's character in *Casablanca*, team professionals will have many analyses of the root causes of a child's behavior and of what is to be learned from our interventions. The important work is to discuss and synthesize those perspectives while interactions with the student are still fresh. Once, in a meeting convened to develop an intervention with a particularly idiosyncratic student, I said, "This is a lot like our work with Harry a few years back." No sooner did I offer that bit of wisdom than hands shot up around the room with a chorus of, "No, this is not like Harry at all." We had never shared our various conclusions about what had caused Harry to be so challenging; with the passage of time, the team was unable to reconstruct the events in Harry's story in order to craft a shared understanding. Our stories are valuable only inasmuch as we collectively construct their meaning and articulate a shared wisdom. Set time aside to tell stories. The learning must be made explicit; we hang in collectively.

I have learned so much from working with our traumatized, neglected, and remarkably alive students and with their teachers. I want to distinguish that sentiment from the idea that, when I am teaching a core curriculum subject, my students are also teaching me. I come to them with an expertise in teaching theory and content knowledge that is beyond their years. I have no doubt who the teacher of the class is. What I learn, the gift to me, is how *this* student and *this* student and *this* student are coming to understand *this* lesson in the varied and unpredictable ways the human mind can work.

To be fascinated with the thinking and growth of each student is a formula for lifelong learning as an educator. Small classes are prime real estate for such adult education.

The teachers in our schools who embody this accumulated education should be treasured and exalted, but too often they work without the resources and support their challenges demand. The admiration they get is often in the form of "I don't know how you do your work," but rarely are these teachers asked to say how they actually do their work, as if the teachers of our most challenging students are in a different profession or possess superhuman qualities. This is a loss for us all, because the accumulated stories of hanging in with our most challenging students are vital to maintaining a diverse and just society. There will be other students like Dean and Charlie in our schools, and for now what works is less a step-by-step program in a box than a sharing of the learned wisdom from hanging in.

How This Book Is Organized

Each chapter of the book explores pedagogical issues through my work with one or two particular students. A couple of the students are composites. All of the students' names have been changed, and some identifying characteristics altered, out of respect for their privacy and their struggles, from which they have not always emerged with the hoped-for success. Those struggles underscore an important lesson: however hard challenging students have been to teach, their lives have been exponentially more difficult to live. I spent many an hour pondering what my schools could do for these students, but then I turned off my computer and rejoined my loving family, in my safe home where the bills had been paid. Many of our students did not have such luxuries.

Each chapter opens with a short summary of the issues that emerged from the work with the given students. The ensuing portraits of the students and description of the evolution of their growth are designed to embed those issues in the complexity of the daily labor of schools. As you read, if you are wondering how the lessons from each story apply to the students in your school, you are on the right path. Interventions that travel unaltered from one challenging student to another are a fool's gold. Please pan for the nuggets that fit your setting.

If it takes a village to raise typical children, challenging children in our villages need their schools to provide critical attention and some very unique structures. Thomas Armstrong (2012) urges us to make schools "positive niches—advantageous environments that minimize weaknesses and maximize strengths and thereby help students flourish" (p. 13). At the end of each chapter in this book, I will suggest approaches for "hanging in" that provide the most consistency and flexibility in developing those positive niches. The approaches are divided into three categories:

1. *For individual students:* Here you will find a variety of suggestions for students who may present similar challenges, and some warnings about the limitations of any given intervention.

2. *For the adult team:* Hanging in with challenging students is an ongoing curriculum for the adults in a school. Here you will find recommendations for the team to develop skills, obtain support, and not lose hope through the ups and downs of the work. You will also find prompts for storytelling.

3. *For administrators:* Administrators have their hands on the gears of a school and exert the most structural, political, and symbolic pressure on the program as a whole. Here you will find recommendations for constructing systems and procedures that give our most challenging students the best chance for success.

Throughout the book are figures offering advice, charts, and forms that I have come back to repeatedly when puzzling over what approaches might be adapted to the challenging student currently stretching our creativity.

I hope this book helps your school team hang in, learn, grow, and appreciate the hard work they do. I also hope for

- An increase in support and funding for the staff and programs that hang in with our most challenging students.
- An appreciation of the potential that rests within each student and the capacity to hold onto the hope when they can't.
- A realization that the expectation to educate every child is a monumental task, the complexity of which we do not understand.
- A commitment to storytelling and to constructing a shared meaning from those stories.
- An invitation to all educators to work with our most challenging students so that you can add your stories to our growing body of knowledge and practice.

1

Toni

Absolutes and Teachable Moments

Schools embody particular minicultures. That is a good thing—when we enter a school, we want to feel that we are in a special place, that we have stepped from the street into an environment that offers students opportunities that they don't experience elsewhere. The confluence of the staff, the community, the history of the program, the physical characteristics of the building and grounds, and the regulations from the government create a unique school culture. That culture and the special opportunities that it generates are secured by the school having predictable rules and expectations, and the adults having predictable emotional responses to student activity. This story centers on a student, Toni, whose needs bring into question which elements of the school's culture are absolute and which can bend.

Challenges for Toni:

- Trauma history
- Substance use
- Learning disabilities and diminished skill set
- History of school failure
- Lack of trust

1

- Racial isolation
- Explosive outbursts

Challenges for the adult team:
- Maintaining caring when verbally abused
- Not holding grudges
- Rethinking absolute school rules
- Maintaining school safety
- Being alert for teachable moments
- Carefully measuring responses
- Developing reliable plans
- Acknowledging student emotions and frustrations
- Communicating as a team

The Capacity to Trust

When Toni came to the therapeutic school for her initial intake appointment, she was too scared to be alone with us, and so was accompanied by her state-appointed social worker. Toni was not a likely candidate for success. The toxic combination of her learning disabilities, her many gaps in basic academic skills, her post-traumatic stress disorder, her persistent marijuana smoking, and her difficulty in trusting others might never allow her to take the healthy risks necessary to succeed. But there was something in Toni's willingness to hang in that was compelling. During our initial conversation, she flashed an occasional bright smile and gave serious consideration to what she was hearing. Her testing reports revealed a keen intellect, now muffled by her many difficulties. Most importantly, her relationship with her social worker hinted at a lingering ability to connect; if she could trust one consistently caring adult, she might trust the school staff and the other students in the school community.

Above all else, the foundation of schools that hang in with challenging students is building trusting relationships—relationships that allow these often overwhelmed young people to try again. Atwool (2006) notes that for students like Toni, success in school will be "unlikely to develop . . . without a relationship with at least one . . . adult in which they feel worthy and loveable" (p. 322).

Toni would need from us the fundamentals we provided all of our challenging students—namely, the six essential elements of hanging in shown in Figure 1.1.

Figure 1.1	The Six Overarching Elements of Hanging In

1. *Exquisite respectfulness:* All students, parents, and educators must be treated with the greatest degree of human dignity and respect, in every room, every activity, and every interaction. This is not easy to do, and so exquisite respectfulness is practiced by all. If we should have a bad moment and speak sarcastically, angrily, or impatiently, we get back to the other person (whether teacher, administrator, parent, and especially student) and apologize. Respect is nonnegotiable. If a doctor's credo is "Above all else, do no harm," an educator's is "Above all else, do not shame the student."

2. *Working from student strengths:* For many challenging students, the hard circumstances of their lives have diminished the fullest range and expression of what they might have been able to do. While teaching these students the skills to manage what is hardest for them, we must recognize any and all strengths that can be building blocks of a successful life. Not every student in the world will reach mastery in trigonometry or Latin or essay writing, but all have strengths and talents. Students must experience school as a generative environment. The sum total of a day in school should not be an overwhelming reminder of what students cannot do. Ensure that all students have a school adult or activity that connects them to their best possible selves.

3. *Opportunity for student reflection:* "Aha" moments of learning are idiosyncratic. Challenging students come to school with jagged profiles of competencies and experiences. There are many lessons about school and life that challenging students have not been able to grasp *yet*. We should be consistently checking in with challenging students about what they are seeing and understanding. In those moments of conversation with a caring adult, students have the opportunity to crystallize a previously elusive notion, to say in many ways, "Oh, I get it now!"

continued

| **Figure 1.1** | The Six Overarching Elements of Hanging In (*continued*) |

4. *Learning from errors:* The path to competency, especially in the social and emotional domain, is filled with missteps. Students will make the same error more than once. We must make sure that consequences for their errors are not damning. Consequences for mistakes (including punishments) should be time-limited and offer a realistic way to regain trust. As much as possible, and as soon as possible after the misstep, offer ways for students to demonstrate and practice the replacement skill.

5. *Allowing multiple interests to inspire diverse solutions:* With challenging students, there is rarely one issue, one stakeholder, one obvious path. The students' struggles affect their educators, their peers, their families, the community at large, and most significantly, their own growth into adulthood. It is important to keep the multiple interests on the table and not get stuck in the trap that in order to satisfy one interest, the others must be sacrificed. The school community will grow by developing a rich menu of strategies.

6. *Working as a team:* No one effectively does the work of teaching challenging students alone for very long. Teachers and professional staff must have multiple venues to vent, ask for advice, brainstorm strategies, and celebrate successes. All educators bring to the work the experiences and skills that may be critical to the success of a single student and to the growth of the programs—make sure that meetings and other forms of communication access the full range of team input. Everyone who works primarily with challenging students should have an ally, a supportive supervisor, a coach.

Toni Reacts

When Toni started at our school, she found the culture created by our six overarching elements disconcerting. As with many students on the verge of dropping out of school completely, she had tried a year or two of public high school and failed to bear up to its anonymity, stress, and the intense social cauldron. Toni often reacted explosively to situations she found stressful or scary. She could look menacing and swear like a sailor. This had gotten her into a lot of trouble at the public high school. At our school, no matter what Toni might say or do (in her case, academically more often *not* do), she was never shamed. Within such an emotionally safe setting, students have a shot at being reacquainted with their strengths and hopes. But could Toni?

Often we thought not. Like other students who have had hard lives, she experienced the staff's boundless friendliness as unsettling. "You all are too nice. I don't like you all saying hello to me every day." She might have been more comfortable if teachers held grudges and rejected her when she stomped away, muttering curses at them on those rough days when we would have to send her home early because she was refusing to comply with any school rules. Instead, the next day the teachers greeted her warmly, ready to start over on whatever lesson had scared her away the day before.

Toni faced other obstacles. She struggled with feeling isolated. Coming from a black and Latino family, she said, "I'm not used to being around so many white people. My perfect school would be all black." She struggled with homework, with required reading, and with math. But her willpower was enormous, and she had an innate ability to discern people's feelings and to attract people to her. She tested everyone with her abrasive language, impatience, her dark moods, and her approach-and-avoidance behavior when asking for help. For instance, a day after Toni flashed us her warm smile and showed us a dance step to a song we had never heard before, she'd burst into class with headphones on, singing loudly, and when asked to put the headphones away and settle into the task at hand, she'd explode: "This fucking school and its fucking rules. You just want to give students shit all day, don't you?"

Putting Behaviors in Categories

One of the key approaches for hanging in with students who display such unpredictable and explosive behaviors as Toni's is to identify which behaviors demand a rigidly consistent response and which behaviors suggest a more nuanced and context-specific response. Ross Greene (1998), in his excellent book *The Explosive Child*, describes three categories of behavior that we used to sift Toni's typical outbursts and to plan our responses: behaviors that are not to be tolerated, behaviors that the school can ignore, and behaviors we choose to respond to as teachable moments.

At one extreme are *behaviors that are not to be tolerated*, mostly because these behaviors threaten the safety or the integrity of the community. In this category for Toni was aggressively swearing at someone. Toni would be sent home for the remainder of the day if she was verbally abusive. The school team all knew the steps to take when Toni displayed intolerable behaviors. No one cherished the expectation to confront her at those times, but knowing that the teachers had each other's backs, and that the administration would follow through without any question, gave each one the strength to set that unwavering limit.

At the other extreme are *behaviors that the school can ignore*, even if other schools or programs wouldn't. Toni was allowed to wear hats and do-rags; in fact, the realization that such articles of clothing for her were not at all gang related but a safe and creative aspect of her sense of self led the school to reexamine all of its policies toward headgear. What Toni wore on her head provided opportunities for conversation and appreciation of her style. Her hats never interrupted the business of learning. Whether or not she wore a hat had no impact on the school's functioning.

Between the extremes of absolute rule adherence and ignoring is the largest category of behavior, those *behaviors we choose to respond to as teachable moments*. These behaviors occur in the vast gray area of context and relationships and so can be molded into opportunities to learn and grow. For Toni, these moments could be crucial in shaping her emerging capacity for self-control. When Toni turned away from teachers and muttered loudly, when she initially refused to follow a direction, when she slammed a book on her desk and declared the work to be "the stupidest thing I have ever been asked to do," the teachers did not have to immediately censure her. They did not ignore the behaviors; to do so would give Toni a false sense of how the world operated. Instead, they gauged each situation in choosing their responses: Toni's overall mood that day, the volatility of the peer group, their own relationships with Toni, the time available to engage with her. Through experience, teachers developed a handful of guidelines for addressing these behaviors; their accumulated wisdom from the decisions they made and the small successes with Toni were critical in Toni's development.

What worked best for Toni was when teachers gave her a quiet minute after her outbursts. The teachers stood close enough to demonstrate attention but not so close as to trigger Toni's fears. When they gauged that the moment was right, the teachers simply acknowledged and put into words what Toni was feeling: "Wow, that made you upset." The message to Toni was that the school was strong enough to weather her emotions. She might glare back, mutter more, walk farther away, but the teachers did not add to her escalating reactions. They let her safely simmer down. In various ways, again context dependent, the teachers would say, "Let's try that again, OK?" The goal was to communicate that she could move on, and that the staff would not hold grudges. Tomlinson (2012) describes this staff approach as "half pit bull and half Mother Theresa" (p. 88). It was one of Toni's strengths that she could recognize those attitudes in the adults.

We developed a form for sorting student behaviors into the three categories and deciding on responses. Figure 1.2 shows this form, which we call the "Specific Behavior Plan," filled out for Toni. The plan reflects shared team experiences and perspectives and represents a team consensus for how to respond. The form is a tool, not a set rule book, and should be reviewed and adjusted as the team gains new insights and the student develops new skills.

The team also asked Toni to reflect on her own behavior, identifying situations that upset her, how she might avoid these situations, and how she might keep calm if she started to get upset. Toni and staff agreed on an escape plan for her, a safe place in the school where she could go to calm down if she lost, or was about to lose, control. Figure 1.3 is Toni's "Get Me Out of Trouble Plan."

The Team Holds the Power

There is no way to overestimate the critical importance of adult teamwork and communication when we have challenging students like Toni. In isolation, teachers can feel like the last soldier on the battlefield, defending modern civilization against the potential chaos of a world filled with unruly teenagers. Toni was seen as one of those chaos-threatening students. She would often display her bad behavior in front of a lone teacher, provoking all of the consequences the adult had available. As a teacher once admitted to me when reflecting on his own emotional buildup and fear of losing control, which had propelled him to become more harshly punitive than he even expected he could be: "Not on my watch were we going to lose the battle!" When teachers have time to collaborate with each other and administrators, the metaphor of war can be put aside, and we can return to the boundless terrain of education.

The shift for Toni's teachers was to see her as a sad and scared person, who had few tools at her disposal, ineffectively trying to get through her day. In her emotionally charged state, Toni did not yet have the cognitive capacity to modulate her behavior; the arousal process took her from stimulus to action in a short period of time (Siegel, 1999). She stomped away from teachers in shame from what she had just said and fear of what might next come out of her mouth.

In contrast, the adults were an organized team, with all the institutional power at our fingertips. With our collective resources, the adults would never lose. Toni's team learned to be like the black-belt martial artists whose strength and training allow them to stay calm in a conflict, knowing that they hold a huge advantage. They rarely if ever need to actually fight; instead, they can educate. Mendler (2012)

Figure 1.2	Specific Behavior Plan

Behaviors that we are responding to as teachable moments:
- Toni shouts out when work is assigned.

What the teacher says or does to shape new behavior:
- Leave Toni alone for a few seconds.
- Say, "Can you tell me in a quiet voice what is hard about this?"

What student can be expected to do when given a prompt:
- Remain silent; no need to talk to teacher immediately.
- Ask for more time to cool off.
- Ask to go to her safe place.
- Talk to the teacher quietly.

Behaviors that demand one consistent response:
- Toni swears aggressively or is verbally abusive.

What the teacher says or does to interrupt behavior:
- "Toni, it is time to go to your safe area."

What is expected of student:
- To go to her safe area as quietly as she can.

Staff who must be contacted:
- The assistant principal, who will meet Toni at her safe area or come to the room and communicate to her the consequences to her actions once she de-escalates.

Behaviors that we are ignoring:
- Toni mutters under her breath.
- Toni puts herself down verbally.
- Toni scowls.
- Toni disregards headgear rule.

notes: "The only way to effectively manage provocative moments is for you, the classroom leader, to stay calm" (p. 49). Toni's teachers stayed cool in the moment, knowing that they worked as a team, and their calm gave Toni the time and space to try again. For Toni's teachers, maintaining calm was supported by four important conditions:

Figure 1.3	Get Me Out of Trouble Plan

Name: <u>Toni</u>

These things can really make me upset:
- Staff standing too close to me
- Not giving me time to stop doing one thing before I have to do another
- Feeling stupid

Ways I can avoid the things that upset me:
- Don't go into class if I am already pissed off
- Do my homework in study hall

Ways I can keep calm when things are starting to upset me:
- Ask to be left alone ("I want to be alone now")
- Listen to music

My escape plan—where I go in school to be safe when all else fails:
- Outside Sandy's office

1. They knew what the absolutes were and what steps would be taken in those situations.
2. They knew they had the latitude and flexibility to work with Toni in situations that were not absolute and that they would not be second-guessed. This assurance gave them the security to discuss how they might nudge Toni's learning even more the next time they were in a similar situation.
3. They knew they could review as a team Toni's specific behavior plan, and its lists of absolute, ignored, and teaching moment behaviors, which evolved as Toni herself developed a broader array of coping skills.
4. They knew that supporting Toni's emotional development was often going to take precedence over developing any particular academic skill. It was not yet time to judge the team's success based on Toni's standardized test scores.

Toni Responds to Our Holding the Hope

We recognized Toni's breakthroughs mostly in retrospect; each was the result of Toni coming back to school day after day and of the staff holding onto the hope. Sandy, her therapist at school, could look Toni in the eye and talk to her in a direct language rarely practiced in social work schools. For instance, Sandy might say, "It's not okay that you dumped all your shit on that teacher." Sandy's wording connected Toni directly to her own emotions because it was the wording Toni used to talk to herself. In those moments, Toni felt heard and understood. After a year and a half, Toni finally allowed her math teacher to show her the steps of long division. One day, when she had dropped all of her books and folders in the hallway, Phillip, a teacher with blonde hair and bright blue eyes, set aside his own pile of papers to help Toni with hers, and she said, "That was the nicest thing anyone could have done for me." When it came time for writing her senior thesis, the school offered Toni the tutorial support of Meg, a soft-spoken Irish girl from the suburbs, and Toni accepted. The two of them sat in the cafeteria, finding a common language to navigate through the 75 note cards and pages of bibliography required to graduate.

As a school administrator, my own relationship with Toni had always been tenuous. More than once, I was the target of her wrath. I watched from afar as she learned to write book reports, went to a job training program off-campus, cochaired the school's weekly community meeting, and truly became a citizen, someone who would contribute, not only to our school, but to the larger community. In many ways, she changed more than any student I have known in my 30 years in the business. One day, in the middle of her senior year, we were walking onto the campus together. I realized I was jealous of the many staff and students who were now in her circle of trust and warm regard. I decided to take a small risk and let her know how much I admired her efforts. I caught up with her and said, "Toni, you have done an amazing job of turning around your life." There was a pause. She eyed me for a moment and then exclaimed in her most boisterous voice, a voice that still echoes in all of our memories, "It's about time, huh?!"

Hanging-In Recommendations and Considerations for Individual Students

1. *Create schedules that maximize students' contact with the adults who are having success building their trust.* Even if it appears to be giving these students something special that they have not yet earned, this extra contact is what they need. Each student has a different capacity to develop trust.

2. *Let staff who have established trust communicate to the student the school's expectations*—what are the most valuable and guarded elements of the school's culture?

3. *Help each student develop simple coping tools for times of heightened emotions* (going to a special quiet part of the school, taking a walk on grounds, controlled breathing). Make a plan for what the student should do in stressful situations. (See Figure 1.3 for a sample plan.)

4. *Work with students to develop a signal for when they need to escape to a designated quiet place.* Something simple like three fingers in the air can be a way of asking for permission to go without having to give an explanation in the moment. Most students who challenge us with eruptions the way Toni did need escapes before they make things worse. We know they cannot change their behaviors overnight. We want to find ways those behaviors have the least effect on the school's functioning.

5. *Don't enforce consequences immediately when de-escalating the situation with a student.* Almost always, the first task with challenging students who are having an outburst is to support them in calming down. Give these students options for correcting themselves or cooling off, if the momentary behavior does not undermine the safety or culture of the school.

6. *Build in time and positive feedback for students' individual accomplishments.* Challenging students like Toni come into school way behind the pack in feeling good about themselves, so don't worry about spoiling them with compliments—that's an unlikely outcome. More likely, your compliments will build relationships that can allow you to tell the truth about all their behaviors.

7. *Don't stop giving sincere compliments when the student seems to be rejecting you*—you are being tested to see if you can hold up to a bit of rejection. Some students will reject you before you can reject them. Don't let their attitude change your attitude of appreciation. They have to know that *you* believe that they can be successful in the culture.

Hanging-In Recommendations and Considerations for the Adult Team

1. *Storytelling:* Share what student you hung in with for the longest time before you began to achieve academic success. What were the pivotal moments? Share what student you hung in with for the longest time before there was a level of trust. What helped you hang in through that time? What were the pivotal moments?

2. *Review all behaviors that require absolute and unvarying responses.* As teachers we make so many complex decisions every day; having clarity about the absolute behaviors we must address reduces the burden of decision making.

3. *Develop specific behavior response plans for challenging students.* (See Figure 1.2 for a sample plan.) Consider which student behaviors might be responded to as teachable moments, based on the context and the time available, and which might be safely ignored. Share results of using the plan and adjust accordingly.

Hanging-In Recommendations and Considerations for Administrators

1. *Identify places where students who are escalating can calm down.* These places should be easily accessed; a student who in the moment has very little ability to calmly ask for help should not have to navigate a complex set of permissions to get where he or she can recover. Make it easy. The school culture will develop its capacity for safety and compassion.

2. *Develop structures that allow staff who are working closely with challenging students to communicate their progress.* Toni's team shared with each other her small successes and evolving abilities. They were all abreast of what had been tried and what would be the next step to target. Teams need time to meet, or technology, to share the latest news.

3. *Review each year the list of absolute rules and consequences and keep them to a minimum.* Certain rules, followed in lockstep, are critical to maintain the school's culture, but sometimes a school's rules have not been reviewed for years and just keep getting reprinted in the handbook. In many schools, teachers arbitrarily treat a lot of rules as guidelines, because the rules are not the best practice in the moment. The professional culture of a school can erode when teachers feel compelled to go their own way in support of a needy student. Administrators can unite a staff around a smaller set of absolute rules—easier to remember, easier to enforce, easier to supervise—and a lot of reasonable guidelines.

2

Charlie and Dean

Creative Transitions

For challenging students, one of the hardest tasks of the school routine is moving successfully from one place in the school building to another. Many individualized education plans (IEPs) identify transitions as areas of weakness for these students, and yet they are often required to make many shifts during the day, which set them up for being disciplined. The stories of Charlie and Dean reveal the difficulty in dealing with transition problems: some are about the physical hurdles in schools, and some are about the atypical hurdles buried within the students.

Challenges for Charlie and Dean:

- Sensory overload
- Impatience
- Impulsiveness and ineffective coping strategies
- Rigidity
- Minimal peer relationships to help bound their impulses

Challenges for the adult teams:

- Being spoken to rudely

- Setting aside time for an intervention
- Keeping the group stable while helping one student

Getting Ready for Charlie

Marie was a high school history teacher, new to our school and new to the profession. I checked in on her as she was setting up her room during staff orientation week. She had placed her desk in the back corner of the room, where she felt it would be least obtrusive.

"You're thinking strategically about the details," I said. "That's what we have to do. But let's put your desk up at the front. From there, you'll have a direct line of sight through the door into the hallway. When students are walking in the school, they'll know we are keeping a caring eye on them; it can help them resist their worst impulses. And if students want to meet with you, and they are shy, they can see you from the door instead of having to step into the room and search for you. We don't want to give the impression that we are hiding from them. We want them to get the message over and over that nothing pleases us more than to be available. They'll see you at your desk, and you can wave hello. Those little waves will make you feel good all through the year. And I have to talk to you about Charlie."

Charlie was diagnosed along the autism spectrum, but no one is a pure model of any diagnosis. All of his teachers still needed to develop an awareness of the collection of behaviors that Charlie demonstrated.

Charlie loved cars. In his bulging, messy pack, he carried a sketch pad for drawing all sorts of automobiles, in great detail. When he heard a fellow student discuss drivers education, Charlie would jump into the conversation and share information about engines and gas mileage and tire specifications. At times his contributions were appreciated, and he developed a couple of friendships with other students who also were fascinated by cars. Other times, he was gently ignored.

Charlie had solid academic skills but could be hyperfocused on a task. This hyperfocus meant that every transition during the school day was a struggle—not just the big transitions from one class period to the next but also the little ones, from entering the room to paying attention to directions to closing his textbook in order to begin to write on a worksheet. He struggled to find the binder where he kept notes and then to turn to a clean page, because that meant passing by so many interesting ideas already in the binder. He'd amiably call out, "Mr. Benson, do you remember this one, the sentence I wrote about circus clowns?" He was always rushed, always behind, always determined to please.

Some days he just fell apart. "I can't do anything. I can't do anything!" he'd moan loudly, his head down. "I can't go to class today. Don't you understand?!" He acted as if walking into the classroom was walking into a torture chamber. "There's just too much of everything!" Charlie had fewer days like these as he matured, and as we all learned ways to help him enter a room: a clearly designated seat with a cushion; a seat near the windows but with his back to them (to decrease distractions from outside and to afford him natural light on his papers); a seat near the pencil sharpener; a reliable and welcoming "Hello, Charlie" from the teacher.

Marie, our new teacher, would have to know all of this. Charlie would need to see from the first day that Marie was in on what worked for him, that she was on the team. She would also have to be alert for ways that she and Charlie could develop their own special bonds and rituals—he had a unique and playful engagement with every one of his teachers.

Marie would need to know about the voice volume scale that we developed for Charlie (see Figure 2.1). Charlie had difficulty hearing how loud he was and was often oblivious to the context of his talking. Telling him to "keep it down" was too vague—how far down was down? One guideline for hanging in with challenging students is to make directions simple and consistent. Number scales can work better than verbal explanations for describing a point in a range

Figure 2.1	Voice Volume Poster

(we'll see a number scale used to communicate emotions in Chapter 3), and we know an image is worth a thousand words. With Charlie's input (he had great ideas for images), we developed the number volume poster, and with that we could say, "Charlie, we're at Level 2 volume now." Some teachers liked this approach so much that it became part of their class culture, a way to give all students a rubric for conversing, one that identified volume levels between the difficult absolute of silence and the anarchic roar of the playground at recess.

Experience the Classroom Through a Student's Senses

I wanted Marie to view everything she did through the lens of Charlie. By asking "How will Charlie do at this point in the lesson, and what cues will he follow?" the class work would go well for everyone. After Marie put her desk in place, she pondered how to set up the student chairs and tables for Charlie. In rows? In small groups? In a big circle?

We discussed the various ways to arrange chairs and tables. For each arrangement, we predicted what Charlie might assume was expected of him. For instance, if asked to sit directly across from a very focused student, he would likely engage that student in conversation, even if what we wanted was for him to take the cue to be silent. If our best prediction of his behavior proved incorrect, and Charlie was alert to everything in the class but the lesson at hand, we would try again. A key in this process was to believe that Charlie had every intention of being a good student—his behavior was out of synch with our expectations because the environment affected him, not because he wanted to be difficult. How would the placement of his chair support his strengths as a learner and mini-mize his weaknesses?

Marie had an "aha" moment: "The tables and chairs don't have to be exactly the same every day. They should be when Charlie walks in the room, to get him oriented. It would be cruel to switch that every day. But once we are settled in, we can make small changes for the lesson."

The biggest challenge for Marie in hanging in with Charlie was the study period right after lunch. Charlie was always revved up from the chaotic stimulation of the cafeteria. He had seen and heard a thousand things. His mind buzzed with stories and potential drawings and important advice and new jokes he needed to share with his peers. Could the setup of her room moderate his behavior and decrease her need to intervene?

Marie considered all the elements of the physical classroom that she could influence—textures, colors, sound, light, scent. She aimed to make her room as soothing as possible. She went for it in ways that no one else in the school had tried. She turned off the overhead fluorescent lights. She put on soft music or the sounds of a babbling stream. She brewed a pot of mint tea. She stood by the door, slowing everyone down by shaking each student's hand and greeting them by name as they walked into this very unusual classroom. When it was time to be quiet, she rang a deeply sonorous gong with a soft wooden mallet; the class developed a routine of listening as long as they could until the last vibration of sound became inaudible. "Best 20 seconds of the day," she said.

It was a wonderful set of interventions. Her room became a special place, even though every teacher could do a version of what she had done. The students responded, in part to the novelty but also to the actual soothing conditions. "It helps me as well," Marie said. "It's a time of day I also look forward to." Students teased her about being a hippie—"I am far too young for that!" she responded.

For most secondary school students, walking into a score of rooms every day is a simple task. For a handful of students—those challenged by sensory stimulation or by trauma or by a learning disability—crossing each threshold is a risk, which they have to take over and over again. Few jobs for adults require us to switch work sites and supervisors every hour, to adjust to a shift in sound and seating and objects and tones so often. The chairs in classrooms are hard, the desks rigid, the lighting harsh. Rooms smell of dry-erase markers and human sweat and antiseptic cleaners. People talk too loudly or too softly, and the pencil sharpener sounds like a dentist's drill. When working with a challenging student, especially those who struggle with sensory overload, you have to ask yourself, "What will make that student want to be in my room? Is my room better than the hallway?"

One More Intervention to Enter the Room

Charlie loved entering Marie's soothing room for study period as much as any other student, but that wasn't the only intervention he needed. He was still so revved up that his voice boomed, and he invariably needed to finish a train of thought aloud with a peer or to tell a joke he had just remembered. He also made a lot of noise until Marie could sit next to him for a moment to help him decide what to work on from his homework list. Marie decided that Charlie needed an even slower and more predictable transition into her room.

The added intervention was that he would be the last student to enter the room. This was nonnegotiable. Marie stood in the doorway, one eye on the rest of the class, her two hands briefly holding Charlie's two hands as he stood in the hallway. There are some students with whom we would never hold hands; some whom we high-five; some who appreciate a quick, firm handshake; and some who let certain teachers put a comforting hand on their shoulder.

To gain entry to the room, Charlie had to tell Marie two things: the work he would take from his binder as soon as he sat down and the joke he would tell the class. The joke telling was Marie's marvelous way of giving Charlie a chance to make people laugh, while adding another sweet ritual for the group. An unexpected side effect of the ritual was that Charlie's entrance into the room became important for his peers, giving him a more secure place in the group. Charlie told Marie about a joke book from home, and he was now carrying it in his backpack. He never forgot to have a new joke ready. She stood with him each day to make sure his transition into that room would likely be successful. He would then enter class, get his work out, and raise his hand to signal to Marie that he was prepared. She rang the gong. As its last echo faded away, she told the class it was time for Charlie's joke, and after it was told to a variety of groans, laughs, and occasional applause, the group knew it was time to settle into their work routines, Charlie as well.

Dean Always Disrupts the Beginning of Classes

Dean also had a terrible time transitioning from one class to another. As a 4th grader, this was a less frequent occurrence than for Charlie in high school, but Dean's volcanic reaction made each change a stress for everyone. He always wanted to be first in line. He stomped and swore when other students were given that position. His teachers felt strongly that being first in line was a privilege for the students, and Dean could not always get that prized position. Even when first in line, he would often push against other students and then race forward, ahead of the teacher monitoring the class; this often provoked other students to race with him, which made him race faster, creating fears of students tripping over each other against the hard linoleum floors or into door frames. In class he was a ball of distracting energy and emotional frailty, often annoying his peers and disrupting the beginning of the lesson. His agitation did not diminish until he could bury himself into the work the teacher assigned. He frequently missed the start of class because he had been unable to behave himself until the lesson was initiated, and had been sent to the principal's office, where he yelled and cried about how unfairly he had been singled out.

We knew a lot about Dean, his difficult family life, his academic strengths and weaknesses. His teachers were working very hard to give him praise as often as possible and to be consistent and uncompromising when he broke important school rules. They knew they had to balance the safety of the class and the smooth functioning of the school with the needs of this very overwhelmed, and overwhelming, little boy.

As the adult team pondered our options, I remembered and shared Marie's interventions for Charlie, in particular the requirement that he wait by the door with her until she determined that it was time for him to enter the room. She would not let him in until she assessed that he was ready. Marie's other students needed her to smoothly integrate Charlie into their functional space.

Don't Ask Students to Do What They Can't Do

Marie's work crystallized a key notion in our group's work hanging in with Dean: don't ask challenging students to do what they can't do. Don't set them up for a failure that will have no redeeming possibilities. In our work with challenging students, we have to accept that they will stumble, periodically regress, make unexpected leaps in functioning, and then still have bad days or hours or moments. But we must not ask them to do tasks that are likely to result in failure. If we knew nothing else, we knew that Dean could not handle the routine of the transitions.

I also remembered Riley, a student I once had in a math class. He asked me to explain how to do a particular equation. I told him the usual way, and he still didn't do the problem correctly. I repeated my directions; he seemed more confused. I tried a different approach, and halfway through my meandering explanation, Riley's expression told me that he did not understand this explanation either. I looked at him—he had reached out for help and still was so lost. I said, "You don't have to do this problem today, Riley. Right now, I don't know how to explain this to you, and that's my job. I have to do some homework tonight to figure this out. It's my failure, not yours. I promise you that I will do my homework and give you a good explanation tomorrow. I promise you that you will get this when I know what I am doing. OK?" Teaching every child, leaving no child behind, is so difficult to do. Too many students internalize a belief that our failure to know how to teach them in the moment is actually their failure to learn. For challenging students, abandoning them to repeated failure is part of what has made them so challenging.

Dean's team decided that our failure to know how to make transitions go well should not continue to be his failure. We decided that he would not make the routine transitions. One teacher said, "I hadn't thought of this before, but it's as if standing in line and waiting are torture for Dean. And going into a room filled with students wandering about to their seats makes him stressed too, in ways we just don't understand yet. It makes sense that he tries to get to the front of the line and race into the room just to get through that difficult part of the day."

Dean Must Demonstrate Readiness

We met with Dean and his mother and told them our plan: while the other students walked to the next location, Dean stayed for five minutes where he was with a member of the teaching team. During this time, he would start the assignment of his next class. (If the transition was to recess, the staff member would play a card game with him.) If after five minutes he was able to be engaged and polite, he could rejoin his class and was walked to the room where his classmates were now seated, organized, and already working. If in those five minutes he could not demonstrate readiness to go to class, he was walked to the principal's office, where he would likely have ended up before we had this plan, but now without a public failure and disruption to the next class getting started. (A big part of this plan's implementation was the buy-in from the staff and their hope that the five minutes spent with him one to one would result in a huge shared benefit for everyone.)

The plan worked immediately, a rare occurrence of guessing right when we didn't truly understand the causes of the problem. The plan revealed that Dean wanted to get to class; there had been a chance that he would be happy to not be in class. Had he shown no motivation to join his peers, that would have told us something else about Dean's struggles, and we would have needed to rethink this strategy; instead, he displayed motivation to do well. Most unexpectedly, he often seemed happy to have those five minutes with a teacher to himself when he wasn't being lectured for being in trouble. His teachers could appreciate his strengths; he could be a "good kid" getting started on his work. Then, at the end of the five minutes, he would enter his next classroom, already focused on the task at hand, while the rest of the class and his teacher had had a few minutes of quiet transition.

Hanging-In Recommendations and Considerations for Individual Students

1. *Assess the sounds, lighting, smells, and textures of the classroom* if a student is having trouble with a transition into a room. Sometimes it is not the task or the type of teacher, but the actual physical environment encountered that is problematic. This is particularly true for students on the autism spectrum. With just a few questions, many students can tell you what is irritating them.

2. *Preserve the student's standing among his peers during difficult transitions by limiting those times.* Charlie and Dean were annoying their peers over and over and preventing the group from settling into its routines. Limit the amount of disturbance our challenging students can cause; the predictable functioning of the group is critical to the functioning of the challenging students who are part of that group. You don't have to remove challenging students from the group after the damage is done, if you can alter ahead of time the conditions of entry.

3. *Consider the arrangement of the desks and chairs* and how it will enhance or inhibit the completion of each task for the student. Practice with the students rearranging the room and reward them for doing it well. This will also help them learn

to alter their learning environments to be more successful in other settings.

4. *Don't tolerate significantly bad behavior.* For Dean's team, as we saw with Toni's team in Chapter 1, vulgar and aggressive language aimed at a person was not to be tolerated and triggered a predicable course of action. Perhaps the team might learn something else about what Dean found difficult, but whether or not they learned anything, Dean had to experience a good dose of calmly structured, reasonable consequences. For Dean, the first step was a trip to an administrator's office and a call to his mother.

Hanging-In Recommendations and Considerations for the Adult Team

1. *Storytelling:* Share what you have done in any setting to make your classroom an inviting place to enter. What have you seen other teachers do that you wish you could do?

2. *Consider ways to soften the sound in classrooms,* adding such features as cushions, noise-reducing headphones, quiet corners, rugs, and foot-tapping bands around the legs of chairs.

3. *Discuss particular transition routines that have been effective* with challenging students and that likely will be comforting to all students. Focus on routines other than the academic "Do Now" activities that teachers often use to start a class.

4. *Support each other in strategically, and temporarily, removing a student before the transition* that routinely causes the student to undermine the functioning of a class. Hanging in with challenging students means helping them save face and allowing their peers to see them as not always irritating. Discuss how to prevent the intervention from being seen as a punishment. Plan who will handle the student in question and who will work with the rest of the student group during each transition of the day. Sometimes a strategy allows one teacher to handle both

the group and the student; sometimes an approach requires extra adult support.

Hanging-In Recommendations and Considerations for Administrators

1. *Make use of occupational therapists* when assessing the sensory stimulation in environments. They have a deeper knowledge base than even many special educators for evaluating what can distract and how to decrease overstimulation.

2. *When budgets allow, buy more individual student desks instead of tables.* Individual desks can be configured in rows, pairs, trios, quartets. Students can face their own desk away from stimulation without displacing others. Form should follow function, and the more flexibility teachers have in arranging seating, the more likely the seating will maximize the learning of a given activity.

3

Rosa

Sitting Together in Silence

Schools are filled with words: instructions, texts, announcements, reprimands, greetings. Schools are equally filled with emotions. At any given moment in a school, students and teachers feel a range of emotions as broad as all of human experience—but schools do not encourage us to demonstrate most of those feelings, even when heartfelt. For many challenging students, learning to live in a diverse world means learning to moderate emotional extremes so that the business of school gets accomplished. Their emotional learning is often a work in progress. The story of Rosa is about the strength of silently hanging in when a student is struggling with emotion and enough words have already been spoken.

Challenges for Rosa:

- Dyslexia
- Moodiness
- History of school failure and retention
- Trauma history

Challenges for the adult team:

- Identifying and appreciating her effort
- Trusting her honesty
- Acknowledging her emotions
- Allowing her time to process
- Working from her nonacademic strengths

Rosa Talks About What She Knows Well

I watched Rosa on her skateboard one day at recess. It was the first step in developing a good working relationship with her. She was graceful and strong. She was more skilled on her board than any of the boys in the playground, who were unsuccessfully trying to complete basic flips. She skated in and around them. The boys bantered back and forth, as 7th graders do, teasing someone who had fallen or calling "Watch this!" and enduring predictable howls of laughter when the trick failed.

On her own, a few yards from the boys, Rosa practiced one maneuver again and again. I didn't know the name of the trick or the series of turns and jumps involved; I assumed she had failed when the board scooted away or she landed awkwardly. She'd grab the board and begin again. And again. And again. Even after she had completed the trick, she did not alter her routine. She kept practicing the move. At one point, one of the boys yelled over to her, "You having trouble doing that? Check this out!" In a moment, he was on the ground. Rosa said nothing, just smoothly glided past him on her board toward where I stood.

"He's a loser," she said to me quietly. "Just all talk." She jumped down on her board. It spun around twice in the air and then landed just where it had been.

"Wow," I said.

"Everyone can do that," she said, looking down.

I pointed at the boys. "They don't seem to be able to do what you do."

"They just talk," she said flatly.

I didn't know anything about skateboarding. I asked Rosa to tell me about the trick I had observed her practicing. As she did, she spoke more than I had ever heard her say before. She told me the trick was complicated and that she occasionally was able to make it work, but she needed to keep practicing until she could do it every time. She wasn't satisfied yet. It took all of my professional experience not to interrupt her with a lecture about how she might be a better reader if she put as much time into reading as she did her skateboarding. She was talking and I needed to listen.

She told me she lived next to a skateboard park, where she worked on her tricks every day. She told me the names of the various tricks she had mastered, each one more complicated than the one before. She said there was an older boy in the neighborhood who was "the best"; he gave her ideas and advice (remembered word for word), which she applied with dedication to her routines. Not once did she boast about her accomplishments.

"I admire anyone who practices to get better at a skill," I said truthfully, finally succumbing to my desire to teach her a lesson. "I admire you. I never knew this about you. I really appreciate everything you just told me. Thanks."

"You're welcome," she answered and for a moment looked up at me. We exchanged smiles.

A complaint I have often heard through the years from challenging students is that they are never understood. The need of every child to be understood, to be listened to respectfully likely has roots in our evolution of survival as social creatures (Siegel, 1999). Listening is a fundamental way to invite a child into the community. It is commonly said that listening is the cheapest concession you can make. In schools, adults listen, but mostly for the answers to our academic questions. We listen to determine what is right and wrong. We listen for opportunities to lecture. It is unlikely a previous school adult had ever listened to understand Rosa's complex study of skateboarding. Her poor school performance through the years had made her the object of our educational improvement plans, the defective model, the one who did not understand—not the one who wasn't understood.

Students Need Competence to Feel Confident

I had my ulterior motives with Rosa, as I always do (we'll see them again in Chapter 4). I wanted her to work harder at academics and to be a better reader. I wanted her to be less susceptible to sudden displays of anger and self-defeating behaviors. I wanted her to look forward to a productive adult life; she knew that she could not earn a living on her skateboard.

I did not doubt that she was learning something critically important by her persistence in practicing on the skateboard. John Holt wrote in his classic book *How Children Fail*, "What some of these kids need is the experience of doing something well—so well that they know themselves, without being told, that they have done it well" (1964, p. 38). Rosa was learning to do something well.

Challenging students often display diminished academic confidence because they have diminished academic competence. It's hard to try again after years of struggle. If they look only at surface skills and test scores, all students who are behind in their academics have evidence to undermine their confidence (Vail, 1994). To change her view of her own potential, Rosa's school would need to be a place that reinforced her strengths, not only as a skateboarder but as a reflective person who had the capacity to self-motivate, which she clearly had. How sad that schools had given her a very different message about herself.

School had never been easy or particularly kind to Rosa. She had already repeated a grade. She read two years below her peers. She was in my study period at the end of the day, but she rarely did her work. She doodled on papers or chatted quietly with her friends. She spoke less than most but was a sharp observer of the school's social scene. I knew that because she would periodically give me a heads-up on a brewing conflict: "You better talk to Malik, Mr. Benson." She'd briefly look me in the eye, nod, and then look down. When I would suggest that she do her homework, she would just keep looking down.

In classes, Rosa's moods shifted quickly. She could be conscientiously engaged (with some of the determination she showed on her skateboard), then sadly withdrawn, then angry, after which she was ashamed of herself. Her moods seemed to change for no apparent reason. This emotional instability is not uncommon in children with a trauma history; Rosa had had an abusive father, who was no longer in the home. She reacted to the perceived threat of pain from poor school performance with a kaleidoscopic array of emotions.

Unfortunately, schools generally respond poorly to student emotions, especially anger. In one school where I have worked, students who responded angrily to a demerit, even if the anger was self-directed, such as a student stamping her foot, automatically received a second demerit for being disrespectful. When asked if a student who reacted to a demerit by crying would also automatically earn a second demerit, the staff at first seemed puzzled by my question—why would a student be punished more for crying? But anger was not OK. When we work with challenging students, we have to allow the students to safely manage their actual feelings. That may simply mean being quiet with them when they are angry, and doing little else. Not ignoring, but bearing witness.

Sit Down and Watch the Students

Bearing witness is hard, particularly with challenging students; we are almost compulsively integrating ourselves into their activities and thoughts. We devise lesson plans, organize the room, give them constant advice, and complete the loop by sharing our evaluations. What many of us forget to do is simply watch our students be who they are in the absence of our interventions. I had been a witness to Rosa's skateboard skills. Given the pressures of required curriculum and crowded classes, in some ways we don't know our students as they know themselves. We persist in defining them through their responses to our plans for them.

We should plan for them, of course. I also urge that we periodically set aside a few moments to solely observe the most challenging students. Literally, sit in your chair, with no papers to mark or e-mails to answer. Watch. Set a timer and watch for two minutes. "Nonverbal behavior is a primary mode in which emotion is communicated" (Siegel, 1999, p. 121), and as Yogi Berra said, "You can observe a lot by watching." As you watch your students, you might note the following:

- When they walk into the room, are they alone? Laughing? Slumping? Alert to the characteristics of the room?
- When they sit, are they comfortable in the chair? Wedged behind the desk? Organizing their books? Checking out who is behind them?
- When they are working on their own, do they look up to think and then return to the task? Are they smiling to themselves? Do they look scared? Rushed?
- When they express emotion, do they say the emotion they are feeling? Do they express it through their physical movement? Do they hesitate to show what they feel?

I learned through observation to predict how one student, Lisa, a depressed teenager, was feeling each day. On her good days, her hair was neatly brushed, her clothes showed a stylish attention to color and fabric, and she said hello to me on her way to her desk. On her bad days, she looked a mess and tried to slip unobserved into class and her seat. It was easy to regulate my interactions with Lisa and to not expect the same level of immediate responsiveness to the class work from day to day. Some days she needed more time and a gentler tone.

To make my assessment more precise and to let Lisa know I was noticing and acknowledging her overall readiness for the business of learning, she and I developed a simple form of nonverbal communication, based on a scale of emotions. I would quietly say to her, "What's today's number?" A number between 7 and 10 (she was invariably well dressed) meant she was having a good day, and I could push her hard to produce. A number between 4 and 6 meant that she was just managing and might need more time to get work done. A number below 4 (when she invariably looked a mess) meant that I should give her a lot of space, and she would let me know when she was ready to work. No other students had to hear this interaction, and Lisa did not have to provide me with an extended verbal summary of her condition.

Lisa was self-aware enough to measure and communicate her capacity to get to work each day; Rosa could not easily identify or predict her own emotional states; they changed so quickly. The moods of trauma victims can rapidly alternate between hyperarousal and numbing, and the often uncontrollable swings significantly interrupt learning. These students are often flooded or, just as often, are empty (Ogden & Minton, 2000). The pace of their thoughts and emotions cycle so fast that they lose their cognitive organization, shut down, and become unresponsive—or they overrespond, their reactions seeming disproportionate to what is going on.

Rosa Tries Her Best to Control Her Anger

I observed Rosa one day in science class. She raised her hand. The teacher did not see her. Rosa patiently kept her hand raised. When the teacher looked up, she responded to another student who had just raised his hand and gave him permission to get a drink of water. "But that's what I wanted!" Rosa snapped angrily. "I had my hand up first. That's not fair!" Rosa was reprimanded for shouting out. She was told to sit quietly and wait for the boy to return, and then she could get her drink. She closed her book, put down her pencil, and stared ahead, her jaw quivering. When she did get her turn, she did not look up as she crossed the room. The door closed with a hard bang as she went to the hallway fountain. I caught the teacher's eye and gave her a signal to just let it be.

Rosa had shouted out and had closed the door loudly. But she also had stayed in her seat, said nothing to make things worse, and walked across the room without distracting others. In those ways, she had done well. I told the teacher that Rosa had waited a long time with her hand up, also a positive sign.

Later in the day, the teacher told me she had spoken with Rosa and apologized for having kept her waiting so long for a drink. "I don't think an adult had ever apologized to that kid before," she said. "When I told her that I was sorry she had waited so long with her hand up, she seemed to melt." She had also told Rosa that she'd seen and appreciated the many good behaviors Rosa had demonstrated, even when she was upset. "You were angry and frustrated," she had said to Rosa. "It's OK to feel all that." Their relationship in class improved steadily following this episode. One-to-one time with a challenging student, when we are not lecturing, can profoundly shift the dynamics.

Hanging in with challenging students often requires teachers to quickly prioritize our most important interests in the moment. In their conversation, Rosa's science teacher chose to focus on Rosa's strengths, to recognize what had gone well. She did not dwell on the public display of bad manners Rosa had impulsively demonstrated—the lesson on manners and patience would best be delivered at another time. There was sure to be another time, cushioned by their successful conversation and connection.

Many young people do not have words for their feelings. They may verbally be limited to "sad-mad-glad" but physically feel so much more. Students who have been traumatized, both at home and in school, can be flooded with emotions and sensations—but not be able to say what they are feeling. They react. When an adult can give the student a name for the feeling, the student can sometimes let go of the behavior, because someone has noticed.

Help Identify the Feelings Driving the Behavior

When you are hanging in with a challenging student, make an effort to identify the feeling a student is experiencing before coaching a behavioral change. Rosa did not know that her behaviors were communicating a strong emotion. A teacher's attention to her primary emotion ("You are really frustrated, huh?") could literally stop her behavior. Rosa then felt safe and understood by the teacher, which was a prerequisite for taking the risk to learn. From her skateboarding, Rosa knew deep inside that she could learn, but she could not easily cope with the strong emotions that emerged when the task was academic.

If a challenging student is not settling down to work (which can manifest in behaviors from complete shutdown to loud moans to persistent chatter), quietly ask about emotional states before commenting on the behavior. You can ask questions such as,

- Are you having a bad day?
- Are you confused about this work?
- You seem angry today, yes?
- Does it all seem too much right now?
- Do you need a couple of minutes to just sit and do nothing?

Sometimes all a student can do in response to a question is nod her head. Sometimes that is enough.

Aligning with the Student's Inner Strength

Soon after the day Rosa told me about her skateboarding, we shared an experience of that silent kind, which cemented our working relationship. She was walking down the hall to class. She was already late, and she was scowling. I moved into her path so that she would have to interact with me. I asked her how she was doing. She said nothing. I asked her if she was ready for class. She said nothing. I told her that she looked really upset. She nodded silently. I had understood.

"Don't go to class yet," I said. "Sit over here." I motioned to a spot on the floor in the hallway. Breaking out of the predictable adult stance, I modeled what I meant by sitting myself down on the floor, a few feet from where I asked her to sit. She paused for a moment and then sat.

"I have no speech for you here, Rosa. I am just going to sit with you until you are ready to go to class, because right now you are not ready. You'd just get in trouble. OK?" She made brief eye contact, nodded, and dropped her head into her hands.

And we sat and sat, in silence. At one point a teacher walked toward us on his way through the school; I said nothing to him. Rosa looked at me, and I calmly returned her look. Perhaps 10 minutes later, two students walked past, and Rosa and I said nothing to them. She looked my way again, and again I said nothing. I had nothing clever or instructive to say. It was dawning on me that I would be sitting there with Rosa for an extended period of time. I had told her I would sit with her until she was ready, and now I had to stand (or sit) by my word.

It was not easy to just sit there, but I knew there was nothing I could say to make her mood pass more quickly. My willingness to be on the floor with her, and not explain our presence there to those who passed by, gave her confidence in my commitment to her—she was not being singled out or explained or admonished. She was just there with me. I was communicating many things to her, perhaps most importantly that I trusted her own capacity to metabolize her feelings (Ogden & Minton, 2000). I was in alliance with the part of Rosa that could self-regulate, the part of her I had witnessed on the skateboard. I was also modeling for her a way to cope with emotions (Wegman & O'Banion, 2013). My experience of watching her determination as she practiced a skateboard trick seemed very significant in my assessment of her ability to hang in.

I inadvertently giggled once. I was thinking about a time when I had not responded to a challenging student in the expected adult manner, because I wanted to force the student to have a personal and unique exchange with me. Gary was an angry and sullen boy, who once swore at me in such a horrific manner that he was suspended from school for two days. What would I say to him when he returned that he hadn't heard before? How could I get him to participate in a conversation? When he came to my office after his suspension was over, I said to him, "Gary, I think anytime a teacher does something you don't like you can call him a . . . ." And here I repeated syllable by awful syllable all the things he said to me. "That's what students should be allowed to do," I told him. He stared at me, dumbfounded, and then blurted out, "You're kidding, right?" "Of course, I'm kidding!" I vigorously responded. "What school would ever have a rule like that?!"

When I giggled, Rosa looked at me. "Sorry," I said. "I just had a funny memory." I looked at the time. "This class is over in about five minutes. How about we stay here, and then you go to your next class?" She nodded. When the bells rang to signal the end of the period, we both stood up. "You did well," I said to her. "You have so much silent strength in you. Are you ready for the next class?"

"Yeah," she said, and added, "Thanks." She made eye contact. I reached out my hand and, not surprisingly, she gave it a strong shake.

Hanging-In Recommendations and Considerations for Individual Students

1. *Suggest words to describe how a student is feeling.* Oftentimes students are feeling a mixture of emotions that they cannot sort or identify, so you might say, "I could see how you would be feeling angry and hurt and very discouraged right now." These emotional states are not exclusive to interpersonal conflicts—a page of long division problems can trigger a host of emotions.

2. *Sit in silence sometimes.* Many students will benefit from the quiet safety of a trusted adult who is nearby. Adults can't fix everything with words and explanations. Be available, but not intrusive.

3. *Help the student separate behavior from emotions.* Many challenging students operate with the belief that a behavior was inevitable because they were feeling a certain way —"I threw the book because I was mad." Honor the feeling first—"You sure were mad. It's OK to be mad." Then address the behavior —"It is not OK to throw books."

4. *Model emotional intelligence, within a professional context.* One of the best techniques is to share positive emotions about the student's behavior: "It makes me feel really good seeing you in your seat." "It is so satisfying to me when you ask for help." "Thanks for holding that door for me. That brightens up my day."

5. *Engage with students through their strengths.* If we truly believe that intelligence is multidimensional, then every person has something he or she does that is noteworthy. Rosa's skateboarding talent was the manifestation of many strengths (physical, intrapersonal, visual). The fragmented nature of schooling may dissuade a student from seeing how her skills in one domain can influence her success elsewhere. We can make those connections.

6. *Introduce the student to an appreciative younger student.* A younger audience can provide recognition for students whom we see as challenging, but they see as magical. Rosa taught younger children in her neighborhood park how to do skateboard tricks. Your challenging students may be good at drawing or reading baseball statistics or making a great sandwich—all talents that can be shared.

7. *Provide opportunities for movement.* Many students' emotions build and build   until they are given a physical release. Recess

may not come often enough, so find ways to let students like Rosa move. Give students a note to take to the office. Ask them to erase the board. Some students do better if they can stand at their desks or pace in the back of the room.

8. *Praise students when they make the effort to communicate their emotional states.* They may not always find the most complex and accurate words to tell you how poorly they are managing. They may not have solutions for how to get through the hard time they are experiencing. What they are doing is taking the risk to trust you, and in those moments, you can learn to trust them.

Hanging-In Recommendations and Considerations for the Adult Team

1. *Storytelling:* Share how you discovered an unexpected nonacademic (social, ethical, personal, artistic) strength in a student. In what ways, if any, were you able to work with that strength?

2. *Brainstorm words that describe emotional states and ways to include them as part of vocabulary building* (irritable, fidgety, sated, eager, cautious); they may be the *most* useful words we can teach.

3. *Share strategies for fostering physical movement in classes.* Some teachers are very comfortable putting on music and dancing with students for two minutes. Others can get up and stretch with students or throw a pillow or a very soft ball around the room.

4. *Facilitate and compare observations of your students at work.* Set up two chairs, away from your desk when students are on task. One chair is for you to sit in and observe, and the other chair is for a student who may need assistance in the midst of the task. Watch them at work.

Hanging-In Recommendations and Considerations for Administrators

1. *Designate a quiet place in the school for temporary retreats,* not earned by good behavior but recognized as the place to go if a student needs a safe place to be quiet (see Figure 1.3).

2. *Be available to cover for a teacher who is de-escalating a challenging student.* It is symbolically very meaningful when an administrator offers to cover a class, for even three minutes, so that the teacher can complete a complex interaction with a challenging student. Designate other faculty that can also be tapped when the need arises. One school I worked with developed a list of available faculty for every hour, in order of whom to call first. This allowed the school to equitably distribute the responsibility and to efficiently get coverage without a long search—faculty knew when they were at the top of the list for a given hour, and when they were at the bottom.

4

Marcus

Adults Always Have
Ulterior Motives

The academic curriculum and the social expectations of our communities support teachers in guiding students to be contributing members of society. We want to help students maximize their strengths so they can hold jobs, pay taxes, and be happy. Watching students mature along that path is one of the great rewards of the profession. The story of Marcus is about a student who doesn't share the goals that adults have implicitly put in place for him.

Challenges for Marcus:

- History of trauma and loss
- Distrust of adults and institutions
- Involvement in drug culture
- Impatience with process

Challenges for his adult team:

- Balancing critical feedback with acceptance
- Depersonalizing his indifference

- Being genuine in emotions and beliefs while maintaining a professional relationship
- Expecting him to do the work

Marcus Unnerves the Adults

Marcus was almost 18 when he got accepted into our school, but he had the credits of a second-semester freshman. He had been on the road with a rock-and-roll band for two years, in part to escape from an abusive father and in part because he never fit into his local high school. When he came back home, broke and disillusioned, he began to see a therapist. Unfortunately, the therapist had a heart attack and died after only a couple of months of working with Marcus. We suspected Marcus had made money by dealing drugs within his punk music world. He intimated that he had gotten in over his head "with the wrong sort of guys" and had to leave his band in a hurry. That's when he came to us.

Marcus looked at the world with a skeptic's eye. He sat on the side of rooms, his long legs stretched out, leaning back in his seat. His dreadlocks were stuffed into a wool cap, and his jeans were filled with rips and holes and random patches. He sometimes did schoolwork, and sometimes he didn't. His skills were good enough to do standard work. He was never impolite when teachers encouraged him to try a task. He would gently nod his head and say, "I know what you mean." When the teacher then responded, "So, you'll give it a try?" Marcus would say, "Let me think about it." On occasion, the teacher talk seemed to work, and Marcus tried harder, but there were no guarantees. More than one teacher attempted to bring him into the fold by letting Marcus know what a potential leader he could be, how the students looked up to him, how the entire class listened when he contributed a spirited opinion during a discussion. Once I'd seen Marcus react to such a speech with a fit of giggles and another time with an indifferent stare.

He unnerved us. We had no sway over him. At the rate he did work, he clearly was not going to catch up in a hurry on credits and earn his diploma. He occasionally showed a flare of frustration halfway through a long math problem or an extended essay. He would rashly ball up his paper.

"This is a waste. How long do we have to do this?" he'd demand, and then just as quickly disengage, as if his brief show of emotion provided the ever eager teachers with a momentary opening into his soul.

"Can I help you, Marcus?"

"No," he'd say, ever so coolly. "I'm fine."

At one team meeting, some of his teachers expressed deep regret that Marcus was so alienated. They worried that his sporadic work output would result in academic failures, further delaying the prized diploma; he would not tolerate being in school until he was 21 years old, which was the likely age of his graduation, given his efforts. Teachers felt that his disregard for his own potential was a cause for all of us to grieve. He wouldn't let us save him. He wouldn't grow up to be the contributor to society that he was so capable of being. One of his teachers gruffly vented his frustration and anger: "He's wasting the taxpayers' money. Taxpayers make an investment in our school, and they should see a return on their investment. I see his potential as much as anyone here. It's a shame."

Marcus Knows I Have Ulterior Motives

As one semester ended and the next began, I lobbied to have Marcus in my English class. There was intelligence in his sarcasm, a sign of strong linguistic skills. He wasn't afraid to share his opinions, and while he could be biting in his criticism, he was never rude. There was something admirable in his individuality. He could be the spark my class needed. I was assembling a cohort of boys for an all-male class. As a group, they were predominantly the "too cool for school" type.

I believed Marcus would be independent enough to challenge any of his male peers if he thought they were less than intellectually honest.

As with many adolescents, Marcus could identify self-destructive traits in others that he could not acknowledge in himself; he could criticize others for actions that he himself sometimes displayed (Nakkula & Toshalis, 2006). That's what adolescents do in their herky-jerky path toward a stable identity. I had once heard Marcus encourage a peer—"Don't waste your time, dude. Just do your work."—and then watched him fail to complete a simple assignment of his own. I was not deterred by such inconsistency. I was more worried about being in a room with a handful of adolescent boys who barely had the energy and self-worth to say their names. Marcus would be my spark plug. And it didn't take but one minute into the semester for him to speak up.

As soon as the boys walked into the class the first day, they asked where the girls were. I told them my idea was to read books about growing up male and to write about that experience in a safe place. But Marcus wouldn't have it.

"I know what you're up to, Mr. Benson. You're trying to make us all into little versions of you."

"No, Marcus, that's not it. This is an English class, and I want you to read great . . ."

He cut me off, "Mr. Benson, adults always have ulterior motives."

I ignored that remark and explained again the academic goals for the course. Marcus watched me warily, leaning back in his chair, his eyes narrowed. The other boys furtively glanced at Marcus for a few minutes, to see if he would provide the entertainment of challenging the teacher, but instead he slipped into his silent protective shell and said no more. This exchange hadn't been a good start for our work together.

I Have to Tell Him More of the Truth

That night at home, while washing the dinner dishes, I was thinking about the class and what to do the next day when Marcus's words rang back hard: "Adults always have ulterior motives." He was right! We always do! We don't want to graduate little encyclopedias—we want so much more for our students, but schools cloak our true goals, hiding them in the standard school subjects. There is a "secondary curriculum" that lies just below the academic one. As we hang in with challenging students, we predicate our success on what we accomplish beyond the standard lessons. Our agenda includes repairing damaged self-esteem, helping those who have failed to take the risk to try again, supporting those who have been beaten down to trust just a little bit and to know whom to trust.

I wanted Marcus to trust me. Marcus was right—I had ulterior motives, and I always had them, and every single teacher I ever worked with or supervised had them. Our students' parents shared these motives as well. They often requested we help their children with secondary curriculum goals—to form attachments, to experience fun, to want a career. (For a full list of these parent-inspired goals, see Figure 8.1) If I was to break through with Marcus and build a more trusting relationship, I had to tell him a greater version of the truth. The challenge for me in doing this was to be professionally authentic, the essential element of building relationships with students (Miller, Jordan, Kaplan, Stiver, & Surrey, 1997). The great psychotherapist Carl Rogers (1961) described the importance of this authenticity:

> If I can provide a certain type of relationship, the other person will discover within himself the capacity to use that relationship for growth, and change and personal development will occur. What is this certain type of relationship I would like to provide? I have found that the more that I can be genuine in the relationship, the more helpful it will be. This means that I need to be aware of my own feelings, in so far as possible, rather than presenting an outward facade of one attitude, while actually holding another attitude at a deeper or unconscious level. Being genuine also involves the willingness to be and to express, in my words and my behavior, the various feelings and attitudes which exist in me. It is only in this way that the relationship can have reality, and reality seems deeply important as a first condition. It is only by providing the genuine

reality which is in me, that the other person can successfully seek for the reality in him. . . . It seems extremely important to be real. (p. 33)

Unlike Rogers, teachers hanging in with challenging students, such as Marcus, are not therapists, but we must behave as therapists; that is, we must provide an emotionally safe environment in which our students can become their best selves, intellectually and emotionally. We, the adults, are the most significant force for honesty and integrity in the classroom. We have to display a professional self that is authentic. This does not mean that we talk about our personal lives—we are not leading students, with details of our lives, into a friendship—but that we share our professional hopes, fears, and expectations with all the passion and sadness and sincerity in us. If we behave professionally so that students trust us and seek to relate to us, we offer them a path to find a healthy place for themselves in the less-than-ideal world the adults are bequeathing to them. Succinctly put, "Relationships are the means and ends to our development" (Nakkula & Toshalis, 2006, p. 95).

But Marcus was not going to discard his alienation quickly. I resolved to go forward with the intention of being more transparent in my thinking and let the chips fall where they may. I got right to it at the beginning of the next class.

"Everyone, listen up. Marcus was right. I have to offer a sincere apology. I do have ulterior motives. He was right and I was wrong." All eyes turned toward him.

"Told you so," he said calmly. Perhaps a momentary smile passed across his lips.

I had his attention. "So, I plan to reveal to you from now on my ulterior motives, which for this class are, in addition to improving reading and writing skills, that you know yourself better, that you know how to have close friendships with your male friends, and that you understand what society is asking of you as a man. How's that, Marcus?"

After a long moment of silence he said, with some suspicion in his voice, "Well, OK, if that's really it." He looked simultaneously pleased to have his theory about adults acknowledged and unsettled that I had truly exposed my motives and that those motives might be acceptable. Of course, now I had to follow through.

Can We Overcome Their Suspicions?

I'd like to say that Marcus blossomed into a trusting and successful student, but he didn't. He did engage with us at times, and he passed a few classes, but the allure of the road and his friends was too great, and he dropped out of our school and was gone. His lesson has never left me—certain evenings, washing the dinner dishes, I see him in my memory, too old for his years, too hurt to be easily persuaded. I think of him almost every time I post goals for a lesson in my classes.

Students have the right to know our goals—all of them. Challenging students, who have experienced adults as unpredictably dangerous creatures roaming their landscapes, have earned the right to be suspicious of us. If these students are to try again, we have to be transparent in our efforts. We have to bridge the distance between us so that they can "connect one mind to another within relationships" (Siegel, 1999, p. 131) and learn. Since Marcus, I have always told students what I was really hoping to teach them—"I want you to be strong and self-reliant and have the tools to build a good life. You need power, and here's where today's lesson fits in. . . ." No trick questions, no manipulations. Marcus was right: all adults have ulterior motives. Our wisest and most hurt students are watching us daily to see if we are worthy of their trust.

Hanging-In Recommendations and Considerations for Individual Students

1. *Allow time—months of time—to build the relationship.* As the saying goes, "If it's been a long walk into the woods, it is going to be a long walk out of the woods." Trust takes time to establish, and you are establishing not only trust in you but trust in

a group—adults—who have hurt some of our students. Allow for approach-and-avoidance behavior.

2. *Help students articulate their own goals*—come to school 9 out of 10 days, pass the course, stay out of trouble with the law, finish a book. Students like Marcus don't automatically share our goals for them or society's goals; having teachers honestly acknowledge that helps build trust. Provide feedback on how they are progressing toward their own goals.

3. *Post goals for lessons.* Give the specific academic skill goal ("use adverbs in sentences") and the larger academic goal ("be better at arguing"). Don't forget to provide the secondary curriculum goal ("know how to get what you want out of life").

4. *Allow for mistakes you'll make* in gauging how much you can push and how much space the student needs. There are no absolute timetables; you will build the relationship by making sincere errors. The errors make opportunities for doing one of the very best things we can do for such students—apologizing. So few adults have stepped up and given hurt students a genuine apology.

5. *Look for the small moments to acknowledge the basic human needs you share with all students.* The needs of Maslow's hierarchy (from food to safety to intimacy to esteem to self-realization) are latent in the most alienated students. The smallest moments, such as helping a student find a missing pencil, can establish a shared goal.

Hanging-In Recommendations and Considerations for the Adult Team

1. *Storytelling:* Share a time you have taken the risk of being extremely honest with a student in a way that allowed the student to be more successful.

2. *Assume the students will and can do the work, despite past work history.* Your optimism and ability to see latent strengths in all

students is in competition with their fears. Every day provides a chance for every student to take a risk with you and do the work. It may take 100 repetitions of you expecting such effort; keep telling your students in both words and deeds that you have not given up on them.

3. *Do not personally respond to a student's indifference or rejection.* Check with other faculty about the status of their relationships with a challenging student who is not responding to you. Most likely you have done nothing egregious and the entire team is in a trust-building phase. Usually there will be one adult who has the first breakthrough. However, be aware that you might have said something in passing that hurt the student. I have had many little breakthroughs with resistant students by asking them, quietly and directly, "Have I done something that bothered you?" If the answer was yes, then I had the chance to do that wonderful thing: offer a sincere apology. Recently, a student who never acknowledged me responded to my question by saying, "Oh no, I hardly ever say hello to any adults." Since that moment, she sometimes says hello to me.

Hanging-In Recommendations and Considerations for Administrators

1. *Identify whatever absolute boundaries the school wants all staff to maintain* in their relationships with students (no home phone numbers, no sharing of faculty discussions) and highlight all the ways faculty are encouraged to work on mutual interests with students (sharing music, working on murals, starting a dance club).

2. *Dedicate times for faculty to speak with school counselors and psychologists* ("Ms. Jones is making appointments to talk with all of Marcus's teachers next week").

3. *Highlight goals of the school's mission statement that do not pertain only to academic achievement* and catalogue efforts toward

those goals as a way to underscore the need for teachers to be more than purveyors of required curriculum. Chart with teachers the various ways they can build professional relationships with all students to meet those goals.

4. *Diversify your access to information about student life.* Identify school activities and leadership roles that do not have to be earned through traditional academic achievement. Invite your most alienated students into discussions and committees. From their place in the school culture, many alienated students have vital insights into how the school operates.

5

Paul

His Chaos, Staff Patience

Being successful in school depends as much on being organized as it does on being smart. The expectation that students multitask begins to increase in middle school and, for some, can reach a crescendo of chaos in high school. Challenging students who cannot plan or follow through find the effort to cope with increasing academic demands, as well as to navigate all the school rules, monumental. The story of Paul is about a student whose learning disability not only gets in the way of his success but also tries the school faculty's patience, compassion, and unity.

Challenges for Paul:

- Disorganization
- Alienation from adult expectations
- Nonverbal learning disability
- Substance abuse

Challenges for his adult team:

- Working with a student's anti-authoritarian attitude
- Persisting despite avoidance of help

- Understanding countertransference
- Accepting a need for idiosyncratic accommodations

Covering Up Disorganization with Indifference

Paul and his friends all got their driver's licenses in a shorter time than usual. They boasted about knowing someone on the inside who made it easy to do. Teachers did not believe them. These guys bragged a lot. They told outrageous stories. They admired a great hustle, and they reveled in getting by authorities. They stood in the hallways of the school, chronically late for classes, laughing as the teachers cajoled them to move along. Their indifference to routines and social norms was irritating.

They were predominantly white males, but very open to integration—integration facilitated by marijuana, alternative music, strange movies, and inside jokes. They were charming—when they weren't being passively indifferent to the schedules and requirements of the school. They were exuberantly friendly to everyone. They thought the liberal social studies teacher was cool, and most of them could dominate a class discussion about politics and social trends with unusual facts and strongly held, though superficially researched, opinions. They did little homework, were sure they didn't need to take notes in classes, and barely squeaked by, or failed, in far too many courses. If part of the mission of schools is to train the next generation to take over the steering wheel of society, this group was sure to steer us into a ditch.

Many in this group of challenging students ended up with a diagnosis of a nonverbal learning disability (NVLD), or executive functioning disorder, or attention deficit hyperactivity disorder (ADHD). These diagnoses cannot be determined by a blood test or an X-ray—they are identified by observable behaviors over a period of time. There are professionals who question the validity of nonverbal learning disabilities, Paul's diagnosis, and would see him as merely a product of a permissive society, a student who required the antidote of rigid adherence to rules, with no excuses and no second chances.

The Struggle to Get from Point A to Point B

Students diagnosed with NVLD, executive functioning disorder, or ADHD have many common presentations, including simply not getting stuff done despite all their apparent strengths. One time I was describing the characteristics of NVLD to one of Paul's friends and his parents. I said, "It is really hard for someone with NVLD to envision and complete a complex task, to get from Point A to Point E by following the steps, moving from Point A to Point B then from Point B to . . . ."

"You mean there's a point B?" the boy interjected. We burst into laughter. And there was the NVLD dilemma: This student knew how to make the joke, clever as he was with language—and if he could make the joke, he must recognize the problem. So why didn't he do better?

Paul was also competent with the spoken word. Once, away from his buddies, in a moment of reflection and frustration at another poor grade, he articulated a classic NVLD burden: "I've always been smart. People told me I was smart from when I was really young. I sit in class and I understand really quick. But I just can't get stuff done when I am out of school. I can't start stuff, I can't finish stuff. So maybe I'm not smart. Maybe I should drop out."

Paul's experience is like that of many similarly challenged students. He began to talk when he was very young. His family was delighted by his vocabulary and by his memory for conversations. He was a bit awkward and clumsy around children his age but a favorite with his teachers. He was a star in the early years of elementary school. He began to struggle with math when the long division algorithm was introduced, and math never came easily again. The shift to middle school was shocking for Paul—his binder was messy, he was forgetting to do homework, he was invariably late to classes, particularly physical education, which required he get to the locker room, change into his gym uniform (when he didn't forget it), and get out to the courts in quick sequence. For many challenging students, the frenetic movement in high school is middle school on steroids.

Call Paul's problem NVLD, or executive functioning disorder, or ADHD. Perhaps Paul had all of them. In any combination, these learning disabilities make meeting the requirements of modern schools tremendously difficult. You won't be successful if you can't plan and follow through. On a given day, Paul had the following homework: short assignments from three classes to complete by the next morning, two big tests coming up that Friday, the first draft of a short research paper due the next week, a novel to finish the same day the research paper was due. Each teacher assigned reasonable work for his intellectual abilities. They did not account for his minimal ability to prioritize, estimate time needed, break down tasks into a sequence of steps, tolerate partial completion of a task and switch gears to the next task that will also be partially completed, keep all the necessary books and papers where they can be reliably found, and check his work against a rubric for excellence before he handed it in. He had long ago given up on being successful in a traditional way. He got stoned, he had friends, and he tried to hold onto what it felt like to be smart by being into big ideas and making clever observations of the hypocrisy of the adult world.

The Team Struggles to Agree on a Plan

And then Paul got his driver's license. Up until then, the school bus had picked him up (when he wasn't so late out the door that the bus took off without him and he ended up using the city busses or hitchhiking to get to school). Paul's dad had an old, barely functional car. He was willing to give it to Paul after Paul convinced him that he would be more likely to get to school on time with his own transportation. Paul's dad told him that he could have the car if the school also thought it was a good idea.

Paul's request provoked a passionate conversation among his adult team. Most everyone agreed that putting transportation into Paul's hands was a chance for him to practice a developmentally appropriate responsibility.

"But what will we say," one veteran teacher warned, "when he comes late and says it is because his mom left him with an empty tank of gas, and his parents were already gone for the day, so he walked to his aunt's house to borrow gas money, and by the time she got him money and he stopped to get gas, he was late, and it wasn't his fault that his mother used his car and left him without gas."

Ah, yes, Paul the hustler, the exaggerator of adult inadequacies. A school bus showed up and left and that was that. Paul and a car and all the world in between his home and the school promised a glut of potential disasters. Talk about getting from Point A to Point B to Point C!

The team chose a hard line. We would give Paul our approval for driving, but we would not tolerate any excuses at all for being late. "Great!" he said. "No problem. No excuses. I get it. It's all on me. Thanks a lot!" It was hard not to feel like we were being hustled, but we had set a very firm expectation.

It took about two weeks for us to have a problem. There was a fire down the street from the school, and all traffic came to a halt. Paul sat in his car, waiting to move, right behind his old school bus. The police finally secured a passing lane and waved the cars through, one at a time. The students in the bus and Paul arrived well after the first period was under way. Paul and his peers burst as one into the school. The secretary gave all the students on the bus excused late passes, but not Paul. For him, there were to be no excuses.

"You have got to be kidding!" he exclaimed. "I was right behind them. It's not my fault at all. I've been doing great. No, you can't blame me for this!" The secretary told him to go to class, and she would pass along his protest to the rest of the staff.

The Team Struggles to Implement Its Plan

Challenging students threaten staff unity. They expose our differences, often cultural and familial, in the areas of discipline and respect for institutions and traditional authority. These challenging students become our fears of the future. They are representing us in our own dramas regarding parents, siblings, teachers, and judges. This is why a student may evoke compassion and engagement in some teachers, yet other teachers may find him irritating and disrespectful.

On the surface, we were only deciding the consequence for this one incident of lateness. Whatever we decided, we would not be putting Paul's future any more at risk than it already was, and we would not be imperiling our standardized test scores. It was unlikely we would ever be asked to decide on a similar set of conditions. But the many heated responses to Paul's situation revealed how our challenging students can become stand-ins for our concerns about schools, about society, about our families, and perhaps about ourselves.

Certainly, we all had agreed to the "no excuse" rule for Paul; at the time we set the plan, the rule made sense. Some of Paul's team vigorously argued that our credibility as adults rested on being firm about what we had said: "How can Paul learn from his behavior if we change the limits and consequences that we so clearly put into place just two weeks ago? Who are we if we don't stand by our words?" Teachers who wanted to excuse this lateness invariably started their statements with, "I don't want to seem like I'm soft, but . . . ," and they sounded soft.

Everyone agreed that Paul was a hustler: he had rarely been willing to take responsibility for his actions. Just as clearly, staff had a lot more riding on the Paul decision than this single event. Factions formed along fault lines that were remnants of previous decisions. Paul was a Rorschach inkblot of far too many concerns. One teacher spoke of the "slippery slope" that we would be on if we didn't hold firm. Another snapped back, "What slippery slope are you talking about? There's no slippery slope if we don't want there to be. That's up to us. Not everything has to be such a big deal."

Recognizing Countertransference

Countertransference is a term from the world of therapy—it basically means you are getting too personally caught up in a situation. Something about your own life and needs is clouding your ability to see the student for who he or she really is, and to do what needs to be done for the student.

Countertransference is inevitable. We have to get involved to be effective. We have to communicate our hope and determination and find within ourselves the wellspring of belief that a challenging student can learn and grow. In this work, we are often operating at the boundary between professional skills and our own ethical, family, and personal values. Our fears for the world and our sense of competency as professionals are very likely to be triggered working with challenging students.

When you notice that a student has taken on an unusual amount of significance for you—triggering more than typical positive or negative feelings—take a step back from the situation. If you have a trusted peer or coach, tell her, "I might be experiencing a little countertransference with this student." If you don't have that outlet, you can simply ask a colleague how he would react to the same situation. These occurrences are potentially a great opportunity to identify your own humanity and to solidify your professional boundaries. Figure 5.1 lists some typical signs of countertransference.

The Team Steps Away from the Table

It is not only important for individual students to examine their reactions, it is important for faculty as well. After becoming heated over the decision about Paul, we took a team time-out. None of the facts of Paul's story were in dispute, and yet we

Figure 5.1	Signs of Countertransference

1. When half the adult team is outraged at the student's behavior and the other half wants to protect the student.

2. When you are sure that you alone can make the difference for the student and you are willing to do the work solo.

3. When you are lecturing the student well beyond what the student can fully comprehend and make use of for personal growth.

4. When you want to make an example of a student.

5. When you want to make more than one significant exception for the student, especially when you may not want to tell the rest of the team about it.

6. When your feelings for a student are so strong that you want to express closeness; for example, giving hugs that you don't give to other students who behave the same way.

7. When you are being harsher with one student than with others because you don't want to seem like you are showing favoritism.

8. When you are irritated by the way a student looks, or talks with friends, or laughs, or sits.

9. When you wish you could take the student home with you.

10. When you want to make extra sure that the other team members dealing with the student do or say things exactly the same way that you are doing and saying them.

were deeply conflicted. In complex and emotional decision-making situations, it is important to step away from the table, to separate the airing of ideas and opinions from the building of decisions. This process can be activated in four critical steps:

1. Bring the critical stakeholders and decision makers together.
2. Share all pertinent information, concerns, and perspectives, without the imperative to come to a conclusive plan.
3. Separate for quiet contemplation and reflection.
4. Reconvene to consider solutions.

Hanging in with challenging students can divide a teaching team the way it can divide parents of these children—and consider that couples who have a child on the autism spectrum are almost twice as likely to get divorced as their peers (Hartley et al., 2010). Teaching these students is not easy work. When people say to me, "It must be so hard to do what you do," I say, "It would be if I worked alone." Being on a committed, interdisciplinary team provides the collective strengths and wisdom that cannot be found in a single person. But there are times, in the heat of a principled argument, when we need to step away. During the time-out from our discussion of Paul, not only did we cool off emotionally, but we found in our silence a chance to rethink and reorganize our ideas.

We reconvened in 30 minutes. Paul's in-school tutor told us that she had sat quietly at her desk. She had pondered, drunk a cup of coffee, and come to a synthesis of many positions:

> We really did say that there would be no excuses. And it is good to stick to what we say. After all, Paul agreed to that decision, too—it was a mutual plan, and he's responsible for his part. And it's not a life-or-death situation, people. He receives one late mark, and that one late mark won't sabotage his life plans. He can learn to accept a consequence like this and move on.
>
> What is equally important is that someone sit down with him and tell him about our thinking on this. One lesson is that he has to accept the consequence of his decisions. But another important lesson is that adults can weigh circumstances and reconsider decisions. We can tell him that if the only reason he loses credit in the course is because of fires and earthquakes, we will revisit the original plan. For now, for this time, he is late.

The Team Shares Its Adult Thinking

I was swayed by the notion of inviting Paul into adult thinking. We were not just faceless authorities operating behind a scrim of bureaucracy; we operated from a complex and ethical set of considerations. Sharing the reasoning behind our decision gave us a chance to confront his us-versus-them stance and still stick to our agreement.

As in many stories in this book, our decision was made within the relentless effort to establish a trusting relationship with each challenging student. Having conversations with students about our decisions was not unusual and actually secured our authority. Paul's tutor volunteered to talk with him. It was one more opportunity for the adults to bond with the part of Paul that wanted a relationship that honored his intelligence. The slippery slope turned out not to be a descent into anarchy but a recognition of mutual responsibility. To his credit, Paul accepted in a mature fashion the how and why of the decision.

Headwinds, as Always with Some Students

Of course, the work wasn't done with Paul. The car event was one good step along his very rocky road to graduation (Benson, 2012). Paul and I were soon at another rough patch in that road. He had been late to my morning class so often that he would lose credit in the course if he failed to show up on time again. I told him that neither fires nor earthquakes would excuse his next tardiness—he had used up all of his late arrival allowance on far too many mundane and self-defeating actions. The next week class started and he was not there. I peeked out the window and saw him furiously pedaling a bicycle up the school driveway, his hair wild, his jacket unzipped and billowing. When he burst into the room with a panicked look in his eyes, I pointed at the clock and said, "I'm sorry. I have nothing to do with this. You're late."

"But Mr. Benson," he exclaimed, "it was headwinds!"

He lost that course. He sat with me later that day, outside on a bench, tears in his eyes. He was not arguing the school rules. Something had shifted. The conflict was no longer between Paul and the adults, but between Paul and himself. The relationship he had with his team was becoming an ally in his struggle to succeed against his own worst habits. That is what can happen when we hang in.

He had many unproductive habits, the result of years of avoidance and hustling. Students with nonverbal learning disabilities often develop dysfunctional habits as they struggle with the details of life. They have trouble processing visual information: maps, schedules, outlines, team sports, metaphors. We describe them as "not being able to see the forest for the trees." For Paul, this weakness presented a huge challenge as he approached his senior research paper needed for graduation.

Every task we accomplish over a long period requires patience and self-confidence. Extended writing tasks also require knowing how one detail fits into the grand scheme and how the grand scheme is developed through the details, the forest and the trees. Paul struggled with sequencing, another element of successful writing (and why he battled with math algorithms). He also could not maintain a vision of the final product while the work was in progress. For all these reasons, Paul's written output never matched his intellectual interests and his abundance of interesting facts.

On to the Writing Plan

For many people, writing is a way to clarify their thoughts and communicate their deepest understandings. For others, writing is a barrier to communicating, a seemingly endless gauntlet of rules and restrictions, a daunting maze of grammar and structures. For some challenging students, the expectation to write across the curriculum is overwhelming, not so much an invitation to share as a minefield to cross. The expectation to write and write and write provokes shutdowns and conflicts. For these students, we offered a writing plan with two significant goals: 1) allowing the student to continue to receive direct instruction to improve written output, and 2) allowing the student to demonstrate understanding across the curriculum in ways other than writing.

We put Paul on the school's writing plan (Figure 5.2 provides a template). Except in English class and with his tutor, he would be

Figure 5.2	Writing Plan

Writing Plan for _____

1. Name of team member who will monitor the amount of writing being assigned to the student and negotiate changes, alternatives, and deadline extensions so the student can manage the work load:

_____

2. Name of team member who will provide direct writing instruction to the student—this person assigns writing with the primary objective to improve writing skills: _____

3. Specific writing skills the student will work on:

_____

_____

4. Alternatives to sustained prose writing that work best for this student to demonstrate understanding of content areas (check as many as work for this student):

___ One-to-one interview with teacher

___ Oral presentation to teacher alone

___ Oral presentation to small group

___ Oral presentation to entire class

___ Video of presentation

___ Poster project with annotations

___ Poster project with oral presentation

___ PowerPoint report

___ Word web with oral explanation

___ List of key ideas in words, phrases, or bullet points

___ Other: _____

5. Date plan will be reviewed: _____

offered alternatives to written output in order to demonstrate his understanding—because he couldn't do it in extended prose. Some team members argued that with this accommodation we were letting Paul get away with something. This hard-line attitude seemed justified when, at random times, Paul produced a solid piece of work.

Challenging students sometimes are not challenging. A combination of sleep, relationships, inherent interest, medication, good weather, and the constellations all being in alignment allows students to have temporary breakthroughs on their path toward competency. Paul lived with this conundrum and the often burdensome responses from his teachers: "Well, Paul, if you could do such good work this time, I will expect this level of work from you from now on." The inability of challenging students to re-create on their own the conditions of success often leads teachers to believe that they are "lazy." Paul handed in those occasional well-written assignments with as much dread as excitement.

At first, Paul's tutor could not identify all the reasons he struggled to consistently write. Writing is such a complex task, and the opportunities for errors in conceptualization, organization, and production are innumerable. She shared with him a long list of potential trouble spots (Figure 5.3) in the writing process. This survey included cognitive, emotional, and social barriers. I have adapted the format to many of the tasks we ask of students. I prefer to go through these lists one to one with a student, but many have filled out the list on their own and then met with me for clarification and problem-solving plans. One student asked if he could score each item, from a "10" if it were a particularly difficult item, to a "0" if it never bothered him. I have since offered this scoring option to students, or used it in my conversation after they have taken the survey.

When Paul reviewed the list, he quickly pointed to one line: "I often go on tangents and don't realize it until I have wasted a lot of time." He said it wasn't lack of ideas that plagued him but too many ideas, ideas that ran from one place to another, all of which seemed interesting, but in the end produced a page of writing that

| **Figure 5.3** | Survey: Why Writing Is Often Hard for Me |

☐ My ideas are too jumbled for me to even know what I am thinking.

☐ I know my ideas, but they all seem equally important.

☐ I need an outline of some sort, and I usually can't develop one.

☐ I often have trouble writing first sentences.

☐ It physically hurts to write.

☐ It physically hurts to type.

☐ I cannot read my own handwriting, and I can't type well.

☐ I often go on tangents and don't realize it until I have wasted a lot of time.

☐ I hate the words that come out; they don't match my thoughts.

☐ My thoughts race too fast to write them down.

☐ My thoughts get confused and jumbled as I write.

☐ My thoughts often dry up completely—I have nothing to say.

☐ What I write usually sounds stupid to me, so I erase/delete it and never show anyone.

☐ Even a rough draft has to be close to perfect for me.

☐ I get hung up on spelling and grammar and lose any flow in my writing.

☐ The whole process will take me so long; I don't even bother to start.

☐ I often get distracted by sounds and sights around me and lose my flow.

☐ I often get so physically anxious that it is like being sick.

☐ I don't know when or how to stop; I'll write and write and write.

☐ I often feel shamed and/or overwhelmed by any teacher feedback.

☐ I can't figure out how to incorporate teacher feedback.

☐ I am afraid other students will see my writing.

even he could not follow. So he didn't even bother to try, knowing that his efforts would be in vain. In a parallel fashion, Paul got lost continually when he was driving. His chronic lateness was not a snub to the expectations of school; it was a mark of his vulnerability. He wanted to get to classes on time as much as he wanted to be a successful student, but without a school that hung in with him, his avoidance, masked by cynicism, would have continued to dominate his development.

The tutor hung in. She worked with him on developing a basic outline of the main ideas in his research paper. They wrote them on her big board in large letters. Then she listened as he talked about all the ideas he had in each area. She wrote the ideas in bullet form on the board. Then they spent a lot of time sequencing the ideas; she required that he defend how tangents fit into the sequence. They had many healthy and intellectually rich dialogues about what thoughts were a good fit. Together they erased the tangents and developed transitions.

The final outline they developed did not resemble any form one would find in a textbook—but it was a coherent clarification of how Paul thought. He was trying, finally, to follow conventions and got support to do so. He was relieved, and the dialogue he and the tutor had engaged in throughout the process was the sort of verbal stimulation that Paul could most easily remember, now supported by a very unusual, but intimately understood "outline." Paul crafted sentences that held only the ideas on the board and completed his final graduate paper.

P.S.: He arrived late to graduation.

Hanging-In Recommendations and Considerations for Individual Students

1. *Give students the opportunity to hear the often complex reasoning behind decisions.* We lose nothing from our authority when we ask, "Would you like to hear the reasons behind our

decision?" Paul was always fascinated by our reasoning. He might argue and question, but the payoff for us was that we were in a dialogue.

2. *Offer alternatives to writing for a select few students.* Writing across the curriculum is a wonderful methodology for most students, but not all.

3. *Appreciate verbal play.* Paul was witty and funny; his irreverence was a manifestation of his thinking, and we wanted to exploit any connection to his thinking.

4. *Decrease visual overload for students with NVLD.* In math, limit the number of problems per page and make the drawings big. With maps, verbally explain the organization; don't assume all students will see the patterns of colors and font sizes. Annotate posters.

5. *Watch out for metaphors and flowery language* (to use a metaphor). Say directly what you mean. Offer nonfiction reading options.

6. *Show interest in student interests and ideas;* engage in their alienation so as to break alienation. Their distance is predicated in part on the distance the adults keep from them.

7. *Help students understand their learning styles.* When Paul's tutor explained the cluster of difficulties associated with NVLD, he was surprised that other people were like him, and that there were well-known accommodations that could help.

8. *Use a student's emerging ability to make plans, agreements, and informal contracts.* Paul didn't always keep them, but he was more likely to care about the outcomes if he was included. Discuss how to incorporate his own goals (use of a car) into the plans.

9. *Make a writing plan for any student who needs accommodation for writing* (Figure 5.2 provides a template). Identify one teacher on the team who is dedicated to improving the writing skills of those with disabilities and then helps determine appropriate writing expectations in all classes, task by task. Share

information about the student's writing stumbling points—gained through experience, observation, or the student checklist (Figure 5.3)—and the student's preferred ways to demonstrate learning. Don't assign simultaneous writing tasks.

Hanging-In Recommendations and Considerations for the Adult Team

1. *Storytelling:* Share which student is making you feel most successful these days, and with which student you are still struggling to make a connection.
2. *Make sure there is someone who is working to connect with every challenging student.* Share the opportunities.
3. *Reflect after sharing perspectives and before decision making about a student.* Watch for developing fault lines in team discussions. When your own reactions to a student are unusually strong, evaluate them against signs of countertransference (Figure 5.1 is a list of these signs).
4. *Watch for adhering to rules for their own sake.* When the notion of a "slippery slope" is invoked, analyze the potential for widespread repercussions. Hanging in with a challenging student means that we have to measure the real risks at hand when we change procedure for that single student. (See the discussion about "bureaucratic ritualism" in Chapter 12.)

Hanging-In Recommendations and Considerations for Administrators

1. *Separate deliberation from decision making at meetings.* Build in breaks and encourage people to go to their offices and classrooms to think on their own. Many will appreciate the advice.
2. *Offer the confidential services of counselors for teachers* who wish to explore the intense feelings a particular student can trigger.

3. *Make clear to teams the* process *for making changes.* Faculty need to understand the process as much as the content of any particular change. The slippery slope may be the loss of predictability in how changes are made. Administrators are the guardians of process.

4. *Let teams know that they can reduce writing assignments* across curriculum for specific students and develop mechanisms for the teaching teams to keep track of the amount of writing assigned to these students.

5. *Convene meetings with parents when a reduction in writing is recommended.* Share with parents the roles they can play in supporting the completion of written tasks and other homework.

6

Cedric

Performing but Not Learning

Working with challenging students, we learn to focus on the positive in the midst of inevitable struggle. We are valiantly optimistic, expanding the narrative of possibility for every child. Who are we to say that this child won't grow up to be an astronaut? The world of education is filled with tales of students who have succeeded beyond the narrow expectations of shortsighted adults. However, we also learn to protect disabled students from being hammered by tasks they clearly cannot do; we are trained to differentiate work before the student can fail. With these two contending goals, defining expectations for an individual student is not always easy. The story of Cedric is about how in our effort to be positive, we can mistake guessing for understanding, and in our effort to protect, we can guard self-esteem to the detriment of learning.

Challenges for Cedric:

- Fragmented academic skills
- Random demonstration of abstract thinking ability
- Limited fund of knowledge
- Trauma history
- Migrant family background

Challenges for his adult team:

- Discerning the differences between effort and outcomes
- Letting go of fear of undermining student self-esteem
- Appraising student potential
- Differentiating basic lessons

Cedric Arrives Without a Road Map

All of Cedric's teachers loved him almost as soon as he started at the school. He had recently moved to the United States from Great Britain "with me mum"; his British accent lent him an air of intelligence. Short, dark-haired, and unassuming, he was immediately labeled "Harry Potter" by his peers, and his calm acceptance of that nickname gained him much social capital. He had a long history of having been bullied, which had contributed to depression and school avoidance.

Cedric's records indicated that he had not only missed a lot of school but had never been a particularly effective learner. All his test scores, from cognitive abilities to academic achievement, were below average, and some scores were well below average. At one point, his school had been concerned that he was suffering from fetal alcohol syndrome. Luckily, that was ruled out. One tester had suggested that he might have elements of Asperger's syndrome. Teacher reports varied widely from fears he had significant cognitive impairments to delight in his work.

Through the years, I have seen the records of many challenging students who tested at low levels because they were suffering from the emotional overload of their lives. It is common to see false scores at the lower end. A student cannot accidentally stumble up into the "advanced" level of an assessment, but many suffering students tumble down into the lowest percentages. There was no pattern in Cedric's assessments; the records would not give us a useful roadmap to clearly defined goals.

Cedric's acceptance into a safe, small therapeutic school where there were a handful of other students with a history of being bullied was liberating to his spirit. He was everyone's best friend right away. He threw himself into the classwork. He kept five sharpened pencils in his binder, three pens, sticky notes, and a box of those little reinforcements for the holes in loose-leaf paper. He did his homework, volunteered to help anyone do anything, and enthusiastically threw up his hand in classes to answer every question. In the first two weeks, his teachers raved about his dedication and work.

I was puzzled. Not by his enthusiasm—we had seen many shy and withdrawn students blossom in a school where they knew they would not be subject to ridicule. I was puzzled by Cedric's unexpected academic accomplishments. Though I was not Cedric's teacher, I decided to observe Cedric in class in my position as administrator.

Guessing and Guessing Is Not Thinking

He *was* enthusiastic. He was willing to take a shot at any question the teacher threw to the class. Between his relentless desire to answer and the distracted habits of his peers, Cedric was dominating classes. What struck me was how very often his responses were uninformed, disorganized, and plain wrong. These answers surprised me, but his teachers surprised me even more. They not only didn't interrupt this routine, they encouraged it.

Here is a typical example of Cedric's behavior in class. The teacher asked a question based on a reading: "What was New York called before the British won control of that colony?"

It's a low-level question, just basic recall. Up shot Cedric's hand. The teacher called on him. Then Cedric paused, slightly panicked. He had volunteered before he had done any thinking. He threw out a guess: "Old York?"

His teacher failed to suppress a smile, and said a slow, "No . . . " But Cedric now had the floor and seemed compelled to get it right. "York?" he tried.

"No. Good idea, though, Cedric."

He smiled broadly and with more enthusiasm stayed on it. "Can you give me a hint?" he asked.

"Remember who had controlled New York before the British?"

"No," Cedric replied. "Who was it?"

"It was the Dutch."

"The Dutch?" Cedric immediately exclaimed. No one else had a chance to break in with an answer. "So, was it called New Dutchland?"

"No, but you are getting closer, Cedric." Cedric beamed. The teacher prompted him. "Do you know the name for the city the Dutch came from?" Cedric shook his head. "Well, they came from the city Amsterdam," the teacher said.

"Oh," Cedric responded, slowly. "So did they call it New Amsterdam?"

"Yes!" the teacher responded. Cedric sat back in his chair. He had participated, his teacher appeared to be happy with his work, and in Cedric's own view, he had figured out the right answer. Later the teacher said to me, "This new kid Cedric is great to have in class. I wish the rest of the students worked as hard as he does."

The next day, the teacher reviewed the material again. Cedric did not remember the former name of New York. Before there was a replay of the dialogue between Cedric and his teacher, a bored peer called out, "It was New Amsterdam." The lesson went on.

All I ever saw Cedric do when answering questions was guess. Occasionally, he guessed correctly (his guessing was invariably betrayed by the question in his tone: "Is it 4?"), and then he would say with delight, "I knew that one right away!" When he wasn't immediately correct, he maintained the teacher's attention until he was led to the right answer.

The Teachers Fear Breaking His Spirit

Cedric had basic skills. In situations where he could take his time, ask questions, and get reassurance, he showed more abilities than his testing indicated, no doubt a consequence of the boost he received from personal attention and human warmth. In class, he asked a variety of questions, a handful of which sparked worthwhile discussions. The teachers rode his waves of energy, which came in guesses and questions and random bits of tangential information, to land him where the right answer was blatantly apparent. The teachers did not want to dampen his enthusiasm. They knew his perfect attendance and daily participation were doing wonders for Cedric, and they feared breaking his spirit. They were working from the perspective that "students are more willing to expend effort in getting and dealing with feedback if they have confidence in themselves as learners," but they ignored the equally important notion that feedback should "foster the belief that that achievement is related to specific strategies, specific kinds of effort" (Brookhart, 2008, p. 21). Cedric's mother, who drove him to school each day on her way to clean houses, told us over and over again how much her son loved coming to school.

To maintain Cedric's love of school, his teachers shied away from setting a crucial expectation: that he think on his own and construct knowledge for himself. In his English class, when others were puzzling through readings to organize a main idea for a composition, Cedric looked lost, so he was given a set of statements from which to choose. His teacher brainstormed with him the details to back his main idea, crafting the language from the fragments of ideas Cedric contributed or guessed at. She coached him to put the ideas into a logical sequence for paragraphs: "Cedric, I think this sentence here should go first in the paragraph, don't you?" When he periodically faltered in his writing, she offered him sentence starters, which he enthusiastically employed, saying over and over, "Thank you so much for helping me." In those moments, he was gratifying to work with. He made us feel good about ourselves as helpers, nurturers, guides.

The responses we receive from students give us a strong sense of who we are as professionals (Nakkula & Toshalis, 2006). Cedric's heartfelt gratitude and ability to follow directions led his teachers to conclude that they were doing the right thing for him; they would keep providing the scaffolding to allow him to complete the assignments, and they would be thanked again. But he was no closer to being able to write a composition independently than he had been before all the interventions. He had constructed almost nothing on his own. One small step at a time, his English teacher had done most of the hard work of decision making.

We Rescue Too Soon and Too Often

This is one of the biggest traps when working with challenging students who do not have a consistent grasp of basic skills—we rescue them. They are rescued before they can experience any more confusion. They are given step-by-step directions, often a required accommodation in their individualized education plans (IEPs), for tasks that require pondering, consideration of alternative routes, and evaluation of methods. Teachers are exhorted to break down tasks, to break them down into the tiniest substep that the student can do independently. The opportunities to construct knowledge, to see the big picture and develop a meaningful concept—what could happen after the student followed the step-by-step directions—are cast aside for the very students who most need multiple opportunities to think for themselves.

In an era of standardized testing and the concurrent expectation to touch on all the content before the tests are administered, we sacrifice the time many students need to idiosyncratically come to understand. To quote Brooks and Brooks (1993),

> Many students struggle to understand concepts in isolation, to learn parts without seeing wholes, to make connections where they only see disparity, and to accept as reality what their perceptions question. For

a good many students, success in school has very little to do with true understanding, and much to do with coverage of the curriculum. (p. 7)

Cedric's enthusiasm and quirky abilities, combined with the teacher's desire for him to succeed on mandated curriculum in a high-stakes testing era, created the illusion of learning. One of Cedric's teachers said it so eloquently: "He is performing, but he isn't learning." Cedric wasn't given the time and space to develop the latent ability he had to ponder. Knowing his challenges, he was rescued at the first signs of stalling. He roamed the lower levels of Bloom's taxonomy, bumping into the answers that the teachers set in his path.

Finding the Entry Point to His Independent Pondering

The teaching team had to manage two major issues that twisted together in Cedric's presentation. The first was their fear that students who have experienced pain and failure are too fragile to experience the stress of learning. The second was that the path to understanding is paved with uncertainty, or as David B. Hawkins puts it, "All of us must cross the line between ignorance and insight many times before we truly understand."

The pivotal moment that resolved this dilemma and redirected our work with Cedric came during a visit to the art room. Students were displaying their paintings and drawings, and the teaching team took a walk to the room during our meeting time. We found Cedric's line drawing of an elevated subway track breathtaking and eye-opening. The art teacher gushed about his development of the composition and his willingness to take chances, erase, and try again: "You just can't do something like this all at once. He had to see the big picture in his mind, then work on the details, and then step back and look at the big picture again. And then back to the details. I gave him books of drawings to leaf through and told him to experiment until he found one that worked for him."

His drawing reset our approach. First, we realized that Cedric was a far more complicated person than we had realized. Like many challenging students, his intellectual profile was jagged, with areas of strength (organization and time management, visualization, attention to detail, social skills) and weaknesses (limited fund of knowledge, poor retrieval of procedural learning). This unevenness is what makes these students difficult to teach: they don't allow us to classify them and settle into a routine of teacher behaviors and expectations (we'll see this issue come up again in Chapter 10). In different settings, they perform differently. They race ahead in certain subjects and lag behind in others.

Cedric's team of teachers plunged into the complexity of one boy's unique development. They collected all the evidence of his strengths and weaknesses, not weighing test scores or a single art project as more important than any other piece of evidence. They decided not to assign Cedric to a category of student types and not to keep hunting for the best label to describe him. He would just be Cedric, and they would bring him closer to the growing edges of emerging potentials. They also began to realize that helping him be right all the time was a charade of helping him.

Teachers committed to more consistently using "wait time" after asking a question; all the students would have the time to formulate answers, interrupting Cedric's habit of guessing immediately. (See Figure 7.1 for ways you can structure wait time and answering so that all students participate in class discussions.) When Cedric answered, teachers would ask him, "Is that a guess?" If he said yes, they didn't maintain a long dialogue with him, only thanked him for guessing. When he wasn't guessing wildly, the teachers said, "Cedric, tell me how you got that answer." Being told that he had to give a reason for his answer decreased his participation, but did not kill it. Most importantly, teachers began to uncover the bare bones of his cognitive processes from his responses, and from there, they could give him small, appropriate challenges. They would climb him up Bloom's taxonomy at every opportunity, at his own rate, because "you cannot change the fact that the human brain is individually wired" (Medina, 2008, p. 69).

He Is Resilient Enough to Meet Higher Expectations

The relationships Cedric's teachers had formed hanging in with him early on proved invaluable to his academic development. He knew they cared for him, and so, as they raised expectations, he trusted them. He was resilient, as are many students whose lives have been a challenge to live. These students are not critically fragile. They have survived much tougher circumstances than being asked to meet higher expectations by a teacher who is caring. The teachers understood that Cedric wouldn't collapse or drop out of school if he were left to think. The most recent developments in brain research backed the teachers' beliefs that Cedric had the capacity to learn and grow in ways that were still emerging:

> When children live in a persistent state of fear, the areas of their brains controlling the fear response can become overdeveloped. These parts of the brain may direct behavior even in situations in which it would be more appropriate for other parts of the brain to be in charge. It is important to note that the areas of the brain active in fearful states are different from those active in calm states, and it is predominantly the areas active in calm states that are required for academic learning. . . . Just as traumatic experiences can undermine the brain's development, good experiences can enhance it. (Cole et al., 2005, pp. 17–18)

Good experiences would come to Cedric from all angles, cushioned by warmth and persistent adjustments to his growth. For instance, in math, his teacher stopped sitting next to Cedric to affirm each of his responses. The teacher developed a way to let Cedric feel safe: "Cedric, I won't let you drown if you can't answer this question, but I am not going to rescue you immediately. I will be back in two minutes to see how you are doing. I will want to know what you have tried." Two minutes became three, then four, then five. Finding one step in the solution process became two, and then Cedric took a cognitive leap and began to work long and hard on word problems.

As Cedric had shown with his art project, he had strength in moving from part to whole to part to whole. It is unlikely this capacity would have emerged had his teachers continued to spoon-feed him every morsel of the processes.

We have to reexamine our tendency to fragment schoolwork into error-proof small steps as a path to understanding. If it is true that "one of our best attributes is the ability to learn through a series of self-corrected ideas," and we developed this ability because our survival depended upon making sense of experiences as they unfolded (Medina, 2008, p. 271), then accommodation isn't what supports long-term brain development. We are helping the student secure a few skills in isolation. Through accommodation, you can get them to perform, but you may not get them to learn.

We were rescuing Cedric before he could experience stress. We were scaffolding him to complete a series of tasks, but simultaneously protecting him from the hurly-burly of learning. If we want each child to climb up every level of higher-order thinking, we must expect it for each child. Often for our most challenging students to develop true understanding, we must not be satisfied when everyone else might be praising our efforts to get them to perform. That's not good enough.

Hanging-In Recommendations and Considerations for Individual Students

1. *Give the student opportunities to sit quietly and look over a specific task.* Use a timer and let the student know you will return when the set time is up.
2. *Don't rescue students immediately.* Ask them what they have noticed in a task before you tell him what you want them to notice.
3. *Ask students to report on "experiments" they have tried in their work* (solving math problems, spelling words, finding answers from a text, organizing data into a table, etc.) before unilaterally

breaking a process into tiny steps. They may demonstrate a more global understanding of the task than you would predict.

4. *Provide models of what a final product of a task looks like,* so the student has a chance to think about the whole and have the opportunity to anticipate the next step while waiting for more directions.

5. *Don't treat wild guessing as a worthy cognitive task.* A great question to ask to assess the thinking of a student is "Are you asking me or telling me that answer?"

6. *Say "I've never heard that answer before. How'd you get it?"* when you are worried that a student's self-esteem is on the line because of an incorrect response.

7. *Always praise the effort to think for one's self.*

Hanging-In Recommendations and Considerations for the Adult Team

1. *Storytelling:* Share a time when you have underestimated what a student was able to do. What events led you to see that you could have expected more?

2. *Bring in all the people who know the student when trying to understand the way the student learns* (art and gym teachers, academic advisors, parents, tutors, therapists). Relying only on the major subject or primary classroom teachers, a team can miss important information. Students can display a wide range of skills in a variety of settings.

3. *Maintain a commitment to not using labels or shortcuts to define students.* Allow all the team to summarize what they have tried with a particular student, what seemed to work under what conditions, and what approaches did not seem to work at all. Allow for idiosyncrasies in learning.

4. *Review testing results and ask, "Does this corroborate what we are seeing or are we seeing something else?"* At many meetings, the conclusions of testers are treated as the final word

in defining a student. Consider testing as just one piece of evidence in the puzzle.

Hanging-In Recommendations and Considerations for Administrators

1. *Ask a tester to provide in-service training on the components of tests*, and how the team can read reports. Cognitive and neuropsychological assessments are a fascinating process, but sometimes the results are not always accessible.

2. *Develop a school expectation at IEP meetings for evaluators to explain how a student performed a subtask that indicated an important ability.* Ask the rest of the team, "Does this match, expand upon, or contradict what we are seeing in the classroom?" Copy the "Summary and Recommendations" section of the evaluation report and staple it to the front of the report for easy access.

3. *Support the team when developing an IEP to be more specific with accommodations.* "Break down tasks into small steps" or "Provide a very structured classroom" do not provide enough information and may lead to scaffolding what students can actually do. Which tasks need to be made into smaller steps and to what end? What specific types of structures help this student learn and not merely behave well?

4. *Provide all the team with a one-page, action-oriented summary of all IEPs.* The summary should cut through all of the required bureaucratic elements and testing recommendations (see Figure 6.1 for a summary template). IEPs are designed to be multipage legal, financial, bureaucratic, and pedagogical documents, and the vital information that teachers need is often obscured by jargon. Make it easy for everyone to find that vital information.

Figure 6.1	IEP Summary

IEP Summary Sheet for Cedric

Goals in current IEP:

- Improve math skills to grade level
- Improve spelling skills to grade level
- Write organized and well-supported essays

Where, when, and with what task does this student do well:

- Loves visuals
- Can work from whole to part—give him versions of final products
- Strong peer relationships—can follow through on his role in groups
- Strong organizational and time management skills—he shows up on time with his stuff

Where, when, and with what task does this student struggle to do well:

- His vocabulary is limited, especially for abstract terms and metaphors
- Long sequences of procedures, such as traditional math algorithms
- Listening for the main idea—will seize on a word or two in an explanation
- Don't assume he knows content knowledge common to his U.S. age peers
- He has been bullied in the past and became isolated

Interventions and accommodations that work—be as specific as possible:

- Have him write down the sequence of steps for a procedure in a section in the front of his binder and remind him the next day to use it as a reference
- Ask him if he is guessing at an answer—if so, thank him for guessing but don't reinforce wild guessing
- Ask him to explain his thinking so he can hear himself and you can correct misconceptions
- Use maps and graphic organizers, but you have to talk him through it

continued

| Figure 6.1 | IEP Summary *(continued)* |

Interventions and accommodations that work—be as specific as possible: *(continued)*

- Use a timer or reference the clock and tell him you will give him a specific amount of time to work on his own before you check back
- He can often draw an idea better than he can write it out

Interventions and accommodations that have not worked or seem to make things worse:

- Long explanations without a visual or him taking notes are too confusing; he'll nod as if he understands

7

Amanda

Guess What the Teacher Is Thinking

Our quiet students who slip by may often keep slipping by with little notice. Because these students are not disruptive or academically incompetent, teachers can easily pass over them. Yet these students may not be simply shy and steady, but rather fearful and purpose-fully withdrawn. For some of our challenging students, the anxiety of performing in school is the dominant experience of their days. Will schools help them overcome their fears and experience what it could be like to excel, to stretch out, to speak up? Amanda's story is about teaching the value of one's own thoughts and providing the freedom to express them.

Challenges for Amanda:

- Trauma and self-abuse history
- Streak of perfectionism
- Ability to hide in the crowd
- Minimal confidence

Challenges for her adult team:

- Safely pulling her out of her comfort zone

- Not shaming her
- Not settling for mediocrity
- Giving her opportunity to experience her own strengths

Avoiding Risk: A Way of Life

Amanda was a polite and hardworking student. She kept her debilitating anxiety at bay by taking copious and accurate notes in a beautiful hand, starting all of her work promptly, handing in all of the assignments, and paying strict attention to whatever the teachers said. She listened to anticipate what teachers might ask next, and when they did ask a question, she thought hard about what the teacher was thinking. And that strict concern for what the teacher was thinking, for the answer that the teacher already knew and wanted to hear, was the biggest impediment to Amanda's success.

Amanda had abandoned any concern for what she herself was thinking. As with many students who have faced too many challenges, learning new things in school is often secondary to not being publicly shamed. The avoidance of taking academic risks, the willingness to let others throw out an answer or a theory, is a particular characteristic of students who have been traumatized, especially of female students who have been traumatized. Brown writes of traumatized women: "One's own suffering arises not from individual deficits but rather from the ways in which one has been systematically invalidated, excluded, and *silenced*" (emphasis added; 2004, p. 464). Even in school, when Amanda was no longer at risk of "life and limb," she could still experience the "precariousness" of her safety (Brown, 2004, p. 466). It was simply safer to be quiet.

Amanda Does Not Believe She Can Construct Knowledge

Amanda thought learning was measured by how many facts she could commit to memory and then regurgitate on demand. The hours she dedicated to studying were rooted in an anxiety-driven hope to not forget what might be on a test. As with far too many students, particularly traumatized girls, Amanda saw knowledge as a commodity that the teacher has access to and that the students gain by hyper-attention. Knowledge was not something Amanda believed that she could construct, but only receive. She was a marvelous and fluid reader of fiction, but a laborious consumer of other texts because she read every page multiple times, stopping after each paragraph to review all the facts. "It's all facts, right?" she would ask, in a mixture of despair and determination. She firmly believed, "If it's nonfiction, then it all is true." There was no differentiating what was important until the teacher declared a passage or point to be so, most often in preparing students for a test. Until she got these directives, Amanda needed to listen and hope she could keep up with everything. (The same phenomenon is described in Chapter 10.)

Amanda's silence was often attributed to her being shy. She was a good student, a good girl. She did her work. In standard classes in a standard school, she was not a problem. She hid the deep, self-inflicted cuts and scratches up and down her arms under pretty long-sleeve blouses and sweaters, there in the back of the room. Amanda was not challenging because she was disruptive to the class; she was challenging because she was hiding in plain sight.

In the intimate confines of a school designed for challenging students, Amanda couldn't hide in the back row. In fact, in this school there were no rows, just large tables that formed a rectangle around which everyone sat. But it wasn't the class size alone that allowed Amanda to grow intellectually. And it wasn't by calling on her to shock her into responding—if you tried this, she would most often say, as she had for years, "I don't know," and further questioning would only exacerbate the flush of her cheeks and the cycle of fast breaths.

The Risks of Answering a Classroom Question

There's a risk in venturing to answer a question that the teacher already knows the answer to. Teachers all have asked this type of question: What is the tallest mountain in Africa? What is an example of foreshadowing in "The Tell-Tale Heart"? What is the tangent of a 37-degree angle? Amanda might have known an answer or a part of an answer, but the very fleeting praise she would receive for being right was outweighed by the fear of being wrong, and then, worst of all, having to explain her wrong answer so that it could be corrected. When another student answered, and the teacher affirmed that it was a correct answer, then Amanda, in the safety of her silence, could write it in her notes.

Teachers can ask as many as 400 questions a day, the majority of which, unfortunately, ask the students to guess what the teacher is thinking (Brualdi Timmins, 1998). We often ask these questions with the intention of assessing the whole group's understanding of basic information, but this intention is never fulfilled when only one student answers. Upon hearing a student respond with that one right answer, Amanda's teacher might turn to the larger group and ask, "Did you all get that?" But Amanda was not about to frantically wave her hand, draw the attention of the whole class to herself, and say, "No, I don't understand." There are not many students who have the confidence to do that, and not many will until schools heed what John Dewey said in 1916, almost 100 years ago: "Were all instructors to realize that the quality of mental process, not the production of correct answers, is the measure of educative growth something hardly less than a revolution in teaching would be worked" (1916/2004, p. 207).

Becoming Fascinated with What Amanda Was Thinking

The goal for Amanda was to support her so that she could give an answer or, more importantly, to expose her thinking even when she wasn't able to synthesize an answer. Expressing her ideas would allow both her and her teachers to understand how she was constructing knowledge. The key strategy in providing this support was to *always* be fascinated by Amanda's thinking. Her teaching team accomplished this in the following ways:

- *In class, her teachers became intrigued by how she was right.* Far too often, students with a wrong answer are compelled to expose their thinking for dissection—"Let's see where you made your error." Amanda would happily have hidden under a rock before she would make herself that vulnerable, so Amanda's teachers seized on when she was right to ask her to expose her methods—"Amanda, I also got that answer. How did you do your work to get that?"

- *On written assignments, her teachers' comments gently nudged her for more of her ideas.* Some students have enough confidence to withstand the implied criticism in the feedback "Not enough information" written in red in the margin. Struggling students have a small buffer to weather criticism. Her teachers put aside the bright red pens. They worked with the elements in Amanda's essays that were already good enough, and made it clear, over and over again, that Amanda was worthy of their interest. In the margins of her papers, her teachers wrote: "I love your answer to Number 4. I was thinking much the same. Tell me more about that."

- *Her teachers avoided asking her the big "why" questions*—Why did the United States invade Mexico in 1848? Why does Holden Caulfield reject his parents? Why does a salmon swim upstream? These "why" questions are at the top of Bloom's taxonomy, not at the entry level where a student can then be scaffolded up. Such top-level questions demand that a student organize the varied causes and then defend them. Instead of asking questions that required such a thorough response, Amanda's teachers asked her and her peers questions that allowed them to contribute a piece of the answer—"Can you tell me one reason the United States might have had for invading Mexico?" Amanda didn't have to organize the entire argument, but could contribute what she did know. When all the reasons the United States invaded Mexico were collected, Amanda could then compare and contrast them and prioritize the most important, both complex processes at the top of Bloom's taxonomy.

Using the above techniques ensured that Amanda wasn't guessing what the teacher was thinking. For Amanda, and for all of our traumatized, silent, insecure, and underconfident students, the first right answer has to be what *they* are thinking. Figure 7.1 lists other ways to structure class questions and responses that place an emphasis on student thinking more than on a single right or wrong answer. As you'll see in this list, wait time is an important element to encourage thoughtful answers from all students, especially those who freeze up from anxiety as did Amanda, or those who jump in before thinking as did Cedric in Chapter 6. Wait time also carries the message "I want to hear your thoughts enough to give you time to figure out what they are." The best way to elicit honest, and therefore always correct, answers is to ask sincerely, from the very heart of pedagogical interest, "What are *you* thinking about this?"

Amanda Feels Safe Enough to Think Out Loud

Amanda began to realize something life altering: her teachers were interested in *her* thoughts. She began to understand that her *own* thinking was what she had to pay strict attention to, because it was becoming safer to do so, the *sine qua non* (essential condition) for students with trauma histories. Guessing what the teacher was thinking turned out to be the shallowest form of thought, an interruption to deep contemplation. Over time, when she had an incorrect answer, she could tell the teacher how she got to it because she was used to telling her teacher how she came to understand many things. In that atmosphere, having the wrong answer was a step on the road to the right answer.

Figure 7.1	Answering Techniques That Support Thoughtful Whole-Class Participation

Class, take 15 seconds to think of your answers. I will go around the room starting at Lindsay and everyone will have a chance to respond. When it is your time to answer, if you want to, you can say, "Pass." If you do so, that's OK. I will come back to you, and you can either give an idea you thought of or say an idea you heard from someone else that you agree with. Or a part of an idea you agree with. So in this way we will hear from everyone.

Class, take 2 minutes to develop an answer to this question. You may write down some ideas in a list, in sentences, in images. I want you to go beyond the first ideas in your head. I will then call on you, one at a time.

Class, this is a great question for everyone to consider. I think you need about 37 seconds on this one. I will tell you when that time is up, and then you should *share your answer with the person sitting next to you.* Then I am going to go around the room—this time, let's start with Andrew and go counterclockwise—and *you have to tell us what your partner gave for an answer.* So listen carefully.

Class, here's the deal with answering this question. Everyone will have 20 seconds to consider. Then I am going to ask Eric and Liz their ideas. Then I will ask Jess and Matt to say if they agree or dis-agree with Eric and Liz. Then I will ask Jenny and Max to add any ideas or reactions. We will regularly do this: one group gives a first response, one group says if they agree, and the third group adds comments.

Class, I am not asking you "Why did the Industrial Revolution begin?" but instead, "What are some of the reasons it began?" You can write a list or sentences. I will start this time with Danielle and have her say one reason. I'll write it on the board. Then Casey will give one reason. Then Eric. And we'll go around the room, collecting ideas, until we run out of them. That way, no one person gives all the answers for the group—everyone contributes. When we collect all the ideas, then I am going to have you work on your own to organize them into . . . .

continued

| Figure 7.1 | Answering Techniques That Support Thoughtful Whole-Class Participation (*continued*) |

Class, JP just gave an answer to the question I asked before I could give you all time to think, so now I want you to consider his answer for 10 seconds. Then thumbs up if you agree with JP, thumbs down if you disagree, and thumbs sideways if you are not sure.

Oh no, class, it happened again—this time Jeffrey answered the question before I gave you all time to think. So, it's "Fist to Five" time. Hold up a fist if you disagree, five fingers if you completely agree, and one to four fingers depending how much you agree. Let's see what we all really think, after 10 seconds.

Class, this is a time I want to let the conversation flow more quickly than usual. There is only one thing you have to do before you give your ideas—you have to summarize as best you can what the person who spoke before you said. That way we know we are listening.

Class, I have a question to ask that you will need a bunch of time to think about and organize your answers, and then we'll share them in some fashion. I put together this graphic organizer, which might help you get all the parts of the answer organized. You don't have to use it. You can sketch an answer, or write a list, or sentences. I am not playing "Guess what the teacher is thinking" here. The only right answer is what you are thinking, if it is organized enough for the rest of us to understand. Here goes. . . .

Amanda's relationships with her teachers, manifested in the types of questions they asked her and the time they took to listen to her as her voice gradually emerged, reflect key elements of resiliency, as characterized by Ungar:

- "First, resilience is the capacity of individuals to navigate their way to resources that sustain well-being;

- "Second, resilience is the capacity of individuals' physical and social ecologies to provide these resources." (2008, p. 22)

Amanda brought to school the latent but powerful capacities to try again and to recognize genuinely supportive adults. The school provided the teachers with the class size and open-ended but rigorous questioning that Amanda required.

Amanda was never the first student to shout out an answer, but when gently prompted she'd say, "This is how I am thinking about it." Her teachers could then ask her to explain the various angles to her ideas and suggest further lines of deliberation. Students are always thinking about something. Amanda, a student with a trauma history, didn't need to guess what the teacher was thinking; she needed to know what she was thinking.

Hanging-In Recommendations and Considerations for Individual Students

1. *Consider a variety of ways to call on students*, so that hearing their names called isn't a shock to their cognitive system. Don't call on students whose attention may have drifted so that they are publicly shamed—no teacher would appreciate being so singled out at a staff meeting. For Amanda, the stress of writing notes and calming her often racing thoughts meant that she occasionally was a step behind, despite her deepest wish to be the perfect student. Catching her unprepared to respond did not heighten her attentiveness. Give even the most attention-disordered students a heads-up to refocus before asking a question.

2. Wait time is essential; let the class sit in silence literally 10 seconds while students ponder and formulate their responses. Amanda appreciated when teachers said, "I am going to ask a question, and I will first call upon Henry, Vic, and then Amanda to get their responses. So let's all be quiet now and think how we want to answer. . . ." See Figure 7.1 for more techniques.

3. *Ask follow-up questions after a student gives her first response.* A tentative answer may indicate a richer set of ideas that need to be gently evoked: "Amanda, you said that maybe Huck Finn wasn't a good friend to Jim. Can you tell us a little more about that? I suspect you have a reason for saying what you did."

4. *Allow students to pass on answering any question.* Students who have been traumatized into silence are most often primarily concerned with safety. They watch how the teacher respects individual styles and assess whether the risks of answering questions are worth it. Knowing they can pass on answering is a safety net that needs to be there all the time. They know they are not going to be publicly humiliated in the class, and the relationship with the teacher grows. That's when Amanda began to add her voice to the class.

5. *Ask for parts of answers, not entire explanations and conclusions.* Probably the most difficult higher-order question to answer for a troubled student may be one of the most common: "Why are you crying?" When you come across a distraught student, try asking for a part of the answer: "Do you know a reason you are crying? Can you tell me one?"

6. *Ask about the thinking behind right answers.*

7. *Allow opportunities for students to share with just one other student.*

Hanging-In Recommendations and Considerations for the Adult Team

1. *Storytelling:* Share how you have supported a withdrawn student in becoming more engaged. What types of questioning strategies do you use to engage all learners?

2. *Discuss Bloom's taxonomy and the questioning possibilities within each order of thinking.*

3. *Explore how to develop a balance between assessing the memorization of facts and promoting students' thinking.* Schools provide the service to society of passing along required facts to the next generation. Teachers often feel the burden of that responsibility especially as reflected in test scores. Discuss the importance of recognizing and encouraging students' thinking.

Hanging-In Recommendations and Considerations for Administrators

1. *Provide teams with an overview of the impact of trauma on student performance.*
2. *Note in teacher evaluations how they support student engagement.* Classes should operate along the continuum from sustained silence for concentration to barely contained exuberance for participation (see Figure 2.1). Observations can include data collection on how many different students speak, how long teachers give students to respond to questions, and the range of questions being asked.

8

Jay and Tito

Decision Making and the Secondary Curriculum

Teachers don't work in isolation from the pressures and expectations of the surrounding world. In every moment we are balancing many interests. Our decision making is rarely absolutely right or wrong. Quite often we must instantaneously weigh what *might be* most advantageous now, as well as for the future, not only for the child, but for everyone else in the school community. This responsibility is one of the things that make teaching a complex profession rarely understood by those outside of the classroom. The stories of Jay and Tito illustrate the innumerable considerations and decisions teachers make in choosing what is best for the individual, for the school, and for society. The stories are also about the uncertainty of the outcomes of those choices.

Challenges for Jay and Tito:

- Limited peer connections
- Fragmented skills
- Lack of future plans
- English as a second language and cultural isolation (Tito)

Challenges for their adult teams:

- Prioritizing among innumerable interests
- Protecting the individual in the group
- Presenting a task that is neither too hard nor too easy
- Decision making in the moment
- Having undeveloped relationship with student

All the Things We Teach

On warm days, when I had a few minutes to spare at lunch, I would grab a ball and head to the school's small basketball court. The sound of my dribbling would often attract students, and we'd have a few minutes together, chatting and laughing as we passed the ball and shot. I was taught that everything we do as school staff is curriculum—these few minutes on the court were a chance to reinforce the daily application of physical education, the social norms of game playing, the appreciation of light and shadows, risk taking, time management, gender roles, geometry, and physics.

Perhaps more important than those lessons, a deeper part of our pedagogy was taking place—what is often called "the secondary curriculum" (see Chapter 4). This is the curriculum inherent in every detail of our interaction with students. From the tone of our voice to our posture, from our responses to students' jokes to the posters we hang in the hallways, everything is curriculum; every moment reinforces, expands, or contradicts everything that has come before it. We are always being watched for clues on how to be an adult.

Those who work in schools are entrusted with developing young people's desire to join and improve our society. We do this in conjunction with families, neighborhoods, government agencies, religious organizations. We don't want a generation of mean-spirited and bitter people to inherit our institutions. I would often say to my students, "I need you guys to grow up wise and organized so that when I am an old man, somebody's keeping the subway running, giving me the right medication in the hospital, and making sure my social security checks arrive on time. I am going to need you guys!"

When we played basketball, I shared and coconstructed with them, as a school authority and much older person, moments of unencumbered pleasure. These shared emotions are essential to building relationships that predict long-lasting connections (Siegel, 1999), both to me as an individual and to the society I am always representing. I also need them to help me experience joy in my work. I need them.

What Parents Say They Want from Schools

Challenging students rarely feel needed. They have too often struggled for years with the tasks and relationships in the most dominant social organization in which we ask them to join with us, school. They don't see themselves as inheriting the comfort and stability of adult roles. In the moments we take to play basketball with them, or talk about a movie we all love, or ask them about their favorite candy or music, or their opinion about an election, we invite them into the adult world and offer them the hope that they may yet be able to carve a space for themselves there. It's not a perfect world by any means, but the rewards of holding a job, having a family, and being physically well are obviously better than loneliness, chronic illness, and jail. Those curriculum imperatives were never far from my thoughts as I gave students a high five for a good pass or grabbed the ball and walked them back into the building when lunch was over. The secondary curriculum was always present in parents' thoughts as well.

Each fall, I would meet with the parents of our newest students. I would ask them, "When your child graduates, what do you most want them to take from their experience at the school? What do you most want them to learn?" For parents whose children were significantly behind in basic skills, they always wanted to see improvement in reading and writing and math. But that was far from all that they asked the school to do. Parents whose children were academically competent never listed curriculum requirements such as "learning to find the surface area of a sphere" or "knowing the atomic number of antimony." Just like the parents of low-skilled students, they wanted more. All parents wanted us to help restore their child's lost motivation, passion, and connections to others.

We kept a list of parent-inspired goals. It is a daunting list, an inspirational list, and a reminder of how much hope parents of challenging students can hold onto. We often used the list to review and assess our own teaching practices—asking how well we were moving toward each goal now and how we might improve. Figure 8.1 is a compilation of the parent requests we charted. Our school would strive to meet these heartfelt expectations by teaching the surface area of spheres and the atomic number of antimony. Students could restore their confidence by correcting the errors they made in calculating that surface area, and they would have the willingness to make those corrections if someone they trusted stood nearby. The primary curriculum is never untethered from the secondary curriculum.

Jay Takes a Long Time at the Board

When teaching challenging students, the secondary curriculum often becomes the primary curriculum on any given day, for any given student. Jay was a pot-smoking, slow-talking, goofy student in my math class. His contributions were rarely helpful, and more than once he responded to another student with an inadvertently snide comment, before retreating into a disconnected silence. He was not well-liked—whatever social capital he had gained for being rebellious was lost through his lack of warmth. One day, for no reason I could discern, he was unusually engaged. With eyes on his paper, his pencil moving, he was on task, completing a set of word problems. I asked for volunteers to show their solutions on the board, and Jay called out that he wanted to do Problem 6. Many students quickly glanced

Figure 8.1	The Secondary Curriculum from Parents

Learning Goal: Please teach my student . . .	How We Do This Now	How We Can Do This Better
To start over when frustrated		
To organize actions so they will lead to accomplishments		
To be happy and experience fun		
To feel passion for (or at least like) something		
To have hope for the future		
To open up socially and make friends		
To participate without fear		
To form attachments		
To delight in doing		
To learn his strengths and weaknesses		
To leave the "woe is me" attitude behind		
To self-advocate		
To want a career		
To not be a perfectionist		
To know it is OK to ask for help		
To gain self-confidence and find inner strength		
To learn to use her many talents		
To understand his ability to make a difference in the world		
To make good choices and decisions		
To separate from her parents in a healthy way		

my way, to see what I thought of Jay's offer. "Go for it," I said. He shambled to the front of the room, in a manner he must have thought was comical but elicited no laughter.

His presentation was a mess. He copied his equations incorrectly from his worksheet and had to erase and rewrite them. He couldn't figure out how to hold his paper and write on the board, so he pulled over a chair and leaned down to read his work, and then laboriously transferred, one digit at a time, his answers for the class to follow. As he did his copying, I could see small errors in his computations, leading to inevitable errors later on. The class was stirring rest-lessly—the time for others to show off their work was disappearing. I still had to distribute and explain the night's homework to keep on schedule. I too was restless.

The class became even more irritated when Jay finally completed his copying and began his explanation. He could not reconstruct his own thinking, even with the computation in front of him. He started and restarted his explanations, recognized an error on the board, made the small correction, and began again. I gave up my intention of assigning homework. I became fascinated both by Jay's inability to complete a coherent explanation and by his obliviousness to the effect he was having on his peers.

Teachers Make a Thousand Decisions a Day

It is said that teachers make a thousand decisions a day, and in that moment with Jay in math class, I had to weigh many options and priorities: Should I interrupt Jay, who had for once volunteered and finally was sharing, in order to move the class along more quickly? Was supporting Jay's initiative the most important move for me then? Should I assign the homework without walking the class through it first? Should I just give up on the homework completely? Should I say something to the class to calm their growing irritation? Was there a way to alert Jay to his situation? Did I have to correct his errors in front of everyone? Did the others see the errors, and did they want me to make the corrections? Did they intuit how I was protecting Jay? Did they take comfort in knowing that I would protect their pride the same way I was protecting Jay's, so they too could feel safe taking risks? Were any of the other students confused by Jay's errors so that I would need to dedicate time to verify their mathematical thinking?

With no absolutely right way to save the moment, I made some decisions: "Jay, let me interrupt for a moment to do some planning. I want to give Jay time to complete his work up here, so we'll skip homework for tonight." This compromise of the primary math curriculum might let the others forgive Jay his bumbling. "I want to work with Jay on this problem, and if you are following along, come up front with me, and we'll make a small group with Jay. If you feel good about your understanding of this problem and the rest of your work, just leave your worksheets on my desk, and you can take five minutes to relax where you are."

Especially when you are hanging in with challenging students, the secondary curriculum must not be ignored. But it is not easy to follow, and it is not absolute. The complex decision making teachers do is only marginally reflected in the scores our students receive on standardized tests. Were test scores my primary concern, and were I to be paid for how my class did on tests, in the absence of their understanding of empathy and community, I would say, "Enough, Jay. You're doing it wrong. Have a seat." The rest of the students could then have done more math, perhaps inched up a notch on their test scores and brought me closer to a pay raise. Not working under those conditions, I aimed for societal goals other than a relentless accumulation of math skills.

Enter Tito, and More Decisions

Not long after that day in class with Jay, I was relaxing on the basketball court, calmly shooting, enjoying a warm moment of an early spring afternoon. The usual students joined me, and trailing behind them was Tito, brand-new to the school. "He was quiet and depressed, spoke English as a second language, and read poorly." He had dropped out of his public high school. He was our only student from a rough-and-tumble Latino neighborhood across town, and we were concerned that he might not easily fit into the school. I knew from a brief conversation that he liked basketball. I didn't know if he had skills or just talked a good game. I tossed the ball to him as an invitation to join us.

In one smooth motion, he caught the ball, elevated into the air, and released a sweet jump shot that swished through the net. "Nice," I said and bounced the ball to him again. He dribbled left, then right, and again shot effortlessly and successfully. "Good move," I said.

"Whoa, Mr. B., looks like you've got competition," one of the veteran students teased me.

"You play?" Tito asked, tossing the ball to me so I could show him my skills.

I tossed it right back to him. "I used to play a lot. Now I just shoot around. I'm too old to keep up with you youngsters."

Tito nodded quietly. He stayed with the group as they took random turns shooting. He was significantly better than the rest of them. He wasn't showing off, and I suspected he refrained from displaying his flashiest and most athletic moves, but even his typical moves impressed his peers. I stayed out of the way, decreasing my participation to rebounding and passing the ball. When lunch was over, I shooed them all back into the building and caught up with Tito.

"You're good," I said. "Did you play on the team in your other high school?"

"I did. It didn't work out." He turned and went to his class.

Tito went to the basketball court every break and every lunch time. Unfortunately, he did not attract any peers to the court. He was too good a player. Other students complimented Tito on his abilities but did not play with him. So he was alone. Tito's isolation, combined with his depression, shaky social skills, and unconfident English, meant that he was forging no deep connections with staff or students. Friendships are perhaps the most critical element in a student's attachment to the school community (Hattie, 2009), and the staff was worried that Tito would buckle under the academic weight without strong social supports to hang in. He did, however, ask me the same question every day: "When are you going to play a game against me?" When I declined, he upped the challenge: "Come on, I'll spot you 8 points in a game to 11."

Considering the Possibilities in the Secondary Curriculum

I was hesitant to play Tito in a game of basketball. What goals from the secondary curriculum would be in the mix when we played? If he was so much better than I was that he could give me 8 points and still win, what part of Tito would be nurtured in such a contest? The best outcome would be that he and I bonded, admiring each other's effort and abilities, and from that interaction, Tito might gain an emotional foothold in the school. The key to that bonding would be a mutual desire to play our best and have a good game. He would learn nothing from beating me with a halfhearted effort; as with every element of the primary and secondary curriculum, growth was linked to effort. If I put aside the time to play, I wanted him to work hard to win.

I had an opportunity to be a male role model for Tito, one who was both an athlete and an intellectual. Maybe through our connection as men competing at a game, I could help Tito hang in as a student (Cleveland, 2011). To gain his respect, I would need to play my best, just as when I read to a class, I read my best. No doubt there would be limits on my ability to be a role model, due to my being much older, white, and from a very different background. But with respect for my game could come a respect for my ability to do math and read, and a way to see that in himself. Of course, those are unreasonable expectations to be achieved from a single game of basketball, but when we are hanging in with challenging students, every interaction is infused with such implicit meaning, with the secondary curriculum of hope. The songwriter Rickie Lee Jones put it well: "You never know when you're making a memory."

I agreed to the game and picked a time of day when we would not have an audience. I had watched Tito when he practiced; I was intent on finding a strategy or two that might help me keep the game close. I had grown up in a city myself and spent more hours in schoolyards than in libraries, and I had done some coaching, so I was able to consider how my level of play might be a good match for Tito. I developed a game plan designed to make him elevate his effort to win. Even with my preparation, I thought that I had perhaps a 10 percent chance of winning, and that would only be if every bounce of the ball went my way. Winning wasn't the point—bonding was.

"Are you sure you don't want those 8 points, Mr. B.?" Tito asked when the time came to play. It was an offer, a tease, and a challenge.

"No, that's not a game," I said. "Let's just go for it."

The Goal Is Not to Simply Make Him Feel Good

My basketball strategy worked as well as I could have expected. Tito's shooting was a bit off, as can happen to the best player on any given day, and my shots were falling in, as can happen to the most mediocre player on any given day. Tito seemed confused by the turn of events, and his limited self-discipline and resiliency came into play, influencing his response. He didn't elevate his game by buckling down and concentrating on his skills, but attempted more and more difficult shots. When these missed and the ball came to me, he didn't spring into action to defend me but became deflated and distracted. A good coach would have called a time-out and given him instructions on how to overcome my strategy. Tito did not have an internal coach in his head to give him good advice.

As the game went on, I downplayed my own success: "Wow, that was a lucky shot," I'd say after I scored, or after he missed, "Keep trying, Tito—the ball just didn't bounce your way that time."

I considered playing poorly on purpose and chose not to. Like the situation with Jay at the board in math class, my options seemed at odds with each other. I felt that Tito would have been unbearably embarrassed if I pretended to play poorly—he would have seen through that charade, and I didn't think my pity would strengthen his self-esteem. As in standard academic classes, giving students work that is obviously too easy does not build their self-confidence: "Thinking that the goal is simply to make students feel good about themselves without concern for academic achievement and competence in reading and writing is a fundamental misconception" (Tatum, 2005, p. 78). I was embodying the curriculum for Tito in my effort and skills, and it was a curriculum within his zone of proximal development.

But not on that day. I scored the last two baskets and won, 11–9. I reached out my hand, and he shook it, his head down. "Tito, you are so good. If we played 100 times, I might beat you 10 of those at the most. Today was just my lucky day. How about tomorrow at lunch, I can show you a couple of things I did? And that shot you hit from the corner there was amazing!"

He shrugged his shoulders and walked into the school. He went home that afternoon and never came back.

Our Record Is Never Perfect

Teachers of challenging students take deep satisfaction from the ones who develop through our curriculum and our relationships. The ones who slip through, like Tito, reverberate in our memories. There was more at stake for Tito in that game than I could have ever known. I didn't get a chance to build his confidence and understanding through multiple repetitions of failure and gradual success, the usual pattern of progress for challenging students (Benson, 2012). The primary curriculum of reading and writing never had a chance.

No teacher and no school has a perfect track record. In my work as a mentor and consultant, the story of Tito and the stories of other students in my experience that did not have happy endings stop me from developing the attitude that the "experts" would always have succeeded. The adults in schools can give each other something vital that Tito didn't have: a connection to a community that gets us through the inevitable days when our shots don't fall, and helps us hang in and try again the next day. We, the adults, can create that resilient community and curriculum for students every day and nurture both in every moment. The required curriculum is a given; the secondary curriculum is what distinguishes us as professionals.

Hanging-In Recommendations and Considerations for Individual Students

1. *Take into account the social and emotional pressures of performing academics for a given individual.* The word "performing" carries the connotation of an audience (classmates) and various evaluators (classmates, teachers, family who will read reports). What you may perceive as a no-risk class activity can have great meaning for a student.
2. *Define the aspects of the secondary curriculum that you intend to infuse into your academics.* Just as with the primary academic curriculum, students are at different skill levels within the secondary curriculum, so adjust your expectations to what an individual student can do with support.
3. *Acknowledge with a student that the two of you have different genders, races, ages, ethnicities.* It is OK to do this. You can ask, "Do you think that makes a difference in how we see this activity?" You don't need to teach about equality and rights when you are uncovering what the individual student believes.
4. *Explain your decisions and weighing of interests.* If you have made a decision in the moment that weighed one student's interest against another's, the next day seek out the students and give them some insight into your decision-making process. You do not have to reveal any confidential information to say,

"I want to let you know that I was thinking deeply about what to do then. Here are some of the things I was considering. . . ."

Hanging-In Recommendations and Considerations for Individual Students for the Adult Team

1. *Storytelling:* Share a time when you made a decision to focus on the secondary curriculum that really helped a student. When have you made a similar decision and regretted where it took you and the students?

2. *Discuss differentiation possibilities that expand the ways students at all skill and ability levels can be challenged in a lesson.* Much of the conversation about differentiation focuses on accommodation strategies for students with disabilities that allow them to access the content. Just as important, lessons can include differentiated *objectives* throughout the range of Bloom's taxonomy. Students with a variety of strengths will encounter work at their level of development. This will protect your most vulnerable students from feeling overwhelmed without boring students who are ready to step up. My experience has been that students almost never choose work that is insultingly easy to do. Hattie (2009) ranks student self-reporting as the most accurate predictor of achievement in his entire analysis of school initiatives, noting that students are "very knowledgeable about their chances for success" (pp. 43–44). When offering a range of choices in a lesson, you can say quietly to an anxious student, "Jennie, when I looked at these tasks, I thought you'd find #8 an interesting place to start. Why don't you give that a look?" Such lessons, with options for tasks at many levels, can help the teaching team understand and develop relationships with new students: Can they make choices? Do they choose work within a comfort zone or do they reach beyond it?

Hanging-In Recommendations and Considerations for Administrators

1. *Review school mission statements for goals that speak to the secondary curriculum* (citizenship, pride in craft, etc.). Find the times and places in the school schedule when those goals are richly promoted. Identify the staff and situations that best help the most challenging students experience success.

2. *Seek training for teams on how to promote effective conversations about racial and economic differences with students.* Consider using only well-established organizations.

3. *Seek software that allows staff to input specific and detailed comments into report cards,* bringing critical recognition to the efforts of students who are hanging in. With the computerization of report cards, the commentary related to the secondary curriculum has often been prepackaged into one-line summaries—"Is a pleasure to have in class." "Works hard." "Should bring clean gym uniform." We can do better than that.

9

Jasmine

The Teacher Stands Still

In this era of standardized testing, many have cried out that we are treating students as widgets in a machine and focusing on teachers as only dispensers of discrete and testable bits of knowledge and skills. The current trend toward long-distance learning further diminishes the belief that skilled teachers have an irreplaceable effect on the experience of learning. But students are humans, and they live in communities sustained not by test scores but by relationships. Our work with challenging students is entwined with deliberately forging relationships. The story of Jasmine is about a student who needs to remain distant from her teacher.

Challenges for Jasmine:

- Overly sexualized sense of self
- Strong emotional reactions
- Ineffective self-advocacy
- Fear of intimacy

Challenges for her adult team:

- Maintaining unassailable professional boundaries

- Providing consistency without rigidity
- Identifying unique supports for a student who needs emotional distance

Jasmine, the Provocateur

In struts Jasmine, a slip of a 15-year-old girl with the makeup, teased hair, and tight clothing of a much older woman. The boys in my class sit up straighter. Betty calls her over so they can sit together. They are old friends from lockup, where they were both brought in by the police for underage drinking. Betty is a marginal student in the class; Jasmine, I soon find out, is simply unpredictable. She is not disruptive, not turning over desks. Sometimes she calls out an answer or an opinion. She has no tolerance for the established rhythms and manners of school. She does not understand why we have a rule against girls doing their nails in class.

In the privacy of the office of her school therapist, she will weep and swear at all the men and women and boys and girls who have done her wrong. Jasmine did cocaine with her grandmother. Her father dressed her up like a cocktail waitress to serve his buddies on poker nights. Teachers asked her questions that she could not answer. Assistant principals threatened her with suspensions and warned her of a dire future should she continue to behave in her provocative ways; it was the dire future Jasmine seemed to be con-sciously making for herself, so all the warnings did little more than confirm how well she was doing.

Sorting through Jasmine's intellectual abilities was one con-cern. Another was her sexually provocative conversations, asides, commentary, and clothes. She came to my school from a residential program in which two male staff had been accused of having sexual contact with students. The investigations did not implicate Jasmine in the activity, but she referenced the scandal often, as if she had been in the know and perhaps more than that. This knowledge, real or exaggerated, gave her an even greater aura of danger and elicited even more attention. "Don't you come so close to me," she warned an innocent and awkward prepubescent boy who bumped into her chair. "I'm not your girlfriend."

The Student Complains About the Teacher

Jasmine freely complained about my lessons, my instruction, the style of my shirts ("Why do they all look the same?"), my explanations of quizzes ("Nothing you said makes sense to me. I still don't get it."). She was telling the truth in those moments. I was not teaching her effectively, yet. She stared at me suspiciously as I offered a detailed review of how to pronounce a word, urging her to look at the big school dictionary splayed open in front of us on her desk, my finger pointing at the words. She said, "You're too confusing," and then turned to the class, saying loudly, "Can anyone here help me understand this stuff?"

It was a blow to my ego, more so because of her vocal declaration of my failure. Hanging in with challenging students is stressful enough without the public criticism. I had worked hard to establish the trust of her classmates; Jasmine's inability to progress with me probably kindled their own memories of such failures. I wasn't the only person who could help them, but in my class, with my lessons, their belief in my competence was critical for taking risks. Invariably, a peer did help Jasmine with the task at hand. What peers could not do was push her beyond her comfort zone. With the distance she insisted upon, I could not create the individual challenges for her that grow out of a free exchange of ideas. If it is true that "the ideal lesson or developmental challenge is situated at the edge of one's knowledge or skill level, thereby requiring the student to stretch her mind" (Nakkula & Toshalis, 2006, p. 11), Jasmine was receiving a very uninspired education in my class.

In an effort to forge an alliance, I made her a bold offer: "Jasmine, it is hard for me to do even my mediocre job when you complain so often about me during class. I am going to stop class five minutes early each day, and you can have the floor and air out your complaints all at once. That way I can hear them—I won't be distracted."

She thought I was kidding her, but I insisted that I was serious in my offer, and she agreed to the plan. When she started to complain in the next class, I reminded her to write down the complaint and that we'd all have time to hear her list at the end of class. The other students were fascinated by the prospect. According to the plan, I stopped the class with five minutes to go. We all turned toward Jasmine.

"Forget it," she grumbled. "You are just weird. This whole idea is weird. I have nothing to say."

Soon after, her school therapist, Ruth, found me in the hall: "Jasmine sure doesn't like you, does she?" Ruth shared with me a friendly smile. "I just heard 15 minutes of her imitating you and complaining about everything you do wrong. It's a wonder they let you teach in this school, isn't it?"

"Thanks, Ruth. What do you think is going on with her?"

"You mean, other than she doesn't like school, doesn't trust adults, and says that her mother thinks you're cute and she should be nicer to you? You're going to have to hang in with this one for a long time. She's sort of smart, in her own way, isn't she?"

Yes, Jasmine was sort of smart in her own way. Jasmine's individualized education plan (IEP) told me many interesting things about her, and I was relieved to see that she scored well on cognitive assessments and that her skills were serviceable, with gaps here and there. Her IEP did not tell me how quickly I could win her trust. Or how I could. Or if I could.

Teaching to a Narrow Range

All students are smart in their own ways. Typical students are smart in many ways. They adapt their learning to a variety of instructional methods and to a variety of teacher personalities. Challenging students have less flexibility—in baseball parlance, they have a small strike zone. If you don't pitch the lesson just so on a given day, it feels as if you have failed. That is certainly how Jasmine understood the situation: I had not taught her correctly. As we hang in with challenging students, one of the most important goals is to help them expand their strike zone, to be able to listen and comprehend information that is not delivered in one narrow way. They are going to need more strength and flexibility to manage the complex rigors of life. But that's the long-range goal. Each day along the way, we have to assess what is possible and predict what is not. When the lesson fails, we know we predicted incorrectly.

To work effectively with challenging students, teachers must spend a lot of time in lesson planning. Hidden in every typical set of class activities are trapdoors and land mines that can cause challenging students to disappear or explode. My job with Jasmine was to anticipate the risky moments in each activity and develop a way around them. This is one reason the regulations limit class sizes of students with special needs—their teachers must know each of them intimately. Regular education teachers will benefit from a meeting with the special education staff to get the details of the idiosyncratic styles of the most challenging students. (See Figure 6.1 for a form that communicates such information.) All teachers will certainly benefit from a conversation with their challenging students. Most students will be relieved to have a teacher give them such attention, and that moment of reaching out can overcome a lot of student fear and resistance. But the issue of intimacy for Jasmine was clearly a barrier to our work, because in Jasmine's past experience, intimacy had been corrupted with sexuality. Her complaints and dismissive tone toward me were her protection.

Many challenging students come from families whose culture of communication and rituals of power and control are atypical:

> Our family of origin taught us what power is and how to deal with it. We learned how to communicate our wants, needs and feelings passively, aggressively, assertively, or passive-aggressively. (Bailey, Christian, Hepler, & Speidel, 2011, p. 18)

Jasmine clearly did not read my patterns of authority and compassion in the ways I wished. The codes she had learned in her family of origin compelled her to see me in ways I could not predict. During my prep periods, I'd think back on what had caused a lesson to fail for Jasmine. Perhaps I had spoken too much, stood too close, or maybe I was too far away. I'd give her work to do by herself, and she would protest that she couldn't work alone. I asked her to meet with me before class, when I could preview the lesson so she could be more confident in what was coming next. "I don't need that," she said emotionlessly. I was failing her.

From training and experience, teachers of challenging students develop a stubborn determination to uncover the hidden formula for teaching every one of them. If Method A doesn't work, you try Method B. If that doesn't work, you try Method C. Perhaps you combine a bit of one with part of another. And if that's not success-ful, there are always Methods D, E, F somewhere to be found in the research. Jasmine's IEP said she needed instructions repeated in multiple modalities. How often repeated? How much time between repetitions? Which modes worked best on Monday mornings? Maybe she needed her directions written in nail polish.

The Teacher Stands Still

I found time to talk with Jasmine's therapist. "Ruth, am I the only one she complains about?"

"Oh, no, she complains about everything, although I hear she is doing well in science. But mostly she complains about you. She says you are even more confusing than ever, like every day is different."

"Well, yes, every day is different, because it's like trying to hit a moving target." It was my turn to complain about Jasmine. "One day, I aim a lesson in this direction, using Method A, and she suddenly has moved over there, where Method B would have been effective. So then I aim there with Method B, and now she's moved to a new location, some strange place where Method C and Method R com-mingle. So I switch my aim, and she's moved again. I keep trying. I am aiming everywhere I can. She won't stand still."

"It sounds like you are both moving all over the place," said Ruth. "I suggest one of you stand still. I suggest that *you* stand still, and let her find you."

Ruth had given me profound advice. I have subsequently used the method of "standing still" with many volatile students and taught it to many teachers. The world for Jasmine was already chaotic and unpredictable. The continual reinvention of my pedagogy was not helping her, even if it had been done with the best of intentions. I had been duly diligent in thinking about her and in examining the ways she had performed. I had read her records, talked to other teachers, talked to Ruth, talked to Jasmine. I had not simply chosen one method (my way or the highway); on the contrary, one of the most important skills in working with challenging students is to do whatever they need to learn. What Jasmine needed was simplicity, safety, and a sense of control. It was time for me to stand still. She could then step safely in my direction, on her own terms. I had to be where she could find me.

I knew some things about Jasmine. She was not so disabled that she could tolerate only one rigid approach to learning. I knew she was quick to speak but much slower to process new information. She was excited by the characters in books, less so by an analysis of the author's techniques. She had a tremendous sensitivity and memory for visual details, such as my shirts. She needed a sentence starter or two to launch into an essay. "Just write them on the board over there," she said, pointing across the room, as I approached. She wanted to be a hairdresser but didn't want to spend time in beauty shops "with all those old ladies." She was sounding more and more like a 15-year-old student.

Keeping a Safe Distance

There was one method I knew worked for her and that was to give her a preview of the next lesson. Through Ruth, I knew that Jasmine identified this as a helpful strategy, which made her feel calmer and ready. The strategy came with a problem—I was not going to be one to one with Jasmine in a room. Whatever emotions and memories I was triggering for her, she had made it abundantly clear that I was to keep my distance. This physical distance was a way to support Jasmine to not panic. I did not want her, in any fashion, to misconstrue my attention to her as sexually charged; I wanted her to concentrate on our school business. I also would not put myself in a position in which I could be accused of doing something I did not do. The guidelines for keeping us both safe from her panic should be followed with any student who has experienced sexual abuse. They include the following:

- In meetings, always give the student options of where to sit, or allow him or her to remain standing.
- Sit at a 45-degree angle to the student so as not to confront her or him directly.
- Never sit or stand between the student and a doorway; always provide the student with an escape route; never close the door.
- In class, sit or kneel when speaking with the student; never loom over the student.
- Start conversations only when the student can see you, not from behind.
- Never touch the student or the student's possessions.
- Never speak of, or make reference to, the student's clothing or body.

I used the guidelines as I planned out how to work with her in class and how to implement the preview strategy. In addition to Jasmine, a couple of other students would benefit from a preview of lessons, and one of those was Jasmine's buddy, Betty. I announced to the class that I would be holding special "office hours" for any students who wanted a complete preview of the next day's lessons. Ruth worked with Jasmine, convincing her to go to my office hours with Betty. Betty had none of the worries about forging relationships with male teachers that Jasmine had; where Jasmine would complain about me, Betty would tease me—"Very nice shirt today, Mr.

Benson. Don't you think so, Jasmine?" Betty dragged Jasmine into office hours. They took notes. They left.

There was one more step in my plans for Jasmine. I needed to tell her that I was going to be "standing still." I had to clearly spell out for her the ways I would help her and the ways I would not, making explicit the guidelines I would be using. I pondered the best time and place to let her know. My hesitancy was that she always had such strong emotional reactions to what I said to her directly—often she could not recall the words I spoke, but only my tone of voice, or the ways I moved my hands as I spoke, or my posture.

Putting the Teacher's Plan into Writing

I decided to write Jasmine a letter. A letter would remove my physical presence from the communication. I typed it as well to remove the personal aspects of handwriting. I edited it to remove adjectives and adverbs and any references to her attitudes. It was more a legal document—a business contract or a court order. I gave it to her when she left class one day, making sure that Betty saw me give it to her, ensuring that the letter would be read. I also alerted Ruth to the plan. I wrote,

> Jasmine,
>
> After reviewing the various methods of teaching, I will be teaching you in the following ways. I will not change my ways unless you ask to have a meeting. If you request a meeting, we can meet with Ruth.
>
> - During office hours, I will write on the board the next class agenda, goals, and important ideas to consider.
> - In class, I will answer your questions when you raise your hand.
> - In class, if everyone is doing quiet work and you want my assistance, I will sit at my desk, and you can sit in the chair next to my desk or stand by my desk.
> - In class, if you need directions clarified, you may always ask Betty if you do not want to ask me. If there is someone else who is helpful to you, you may ask that person.

- If you need to meet with me outside of class, you may always bring along Betty or another student. You may also ask for us to meet in Ruth's office.
- If I have any concerns about your classwork, I will write to you. You may show the letter to anyone you wish or throw it out.
- You may write to me as well.

Yours truly,

Mr. Benson

Jasmine did not acknowledge the letter. Ruth told me that Jasmine took it as more evidence of how weird I was, but she also understood what I wrote and said that she would make it through the semester.

Jasmine stopped coming to my office hours, but I think Betty gave her notes. For her part, Betty warmed up to me, an unexpected side effect. Betty could acknowledge that I had tried really hard to help her buddy, even if Jasmine couldn't admit it. But I never talked to Betty about Jasmine, even when Betty complained to me about Jasmine's attitudes. I did not want Betty to feel pressure to divide her loyalties. She and Jasmine needed to trust each other, and they needed that almost desperately, far more than I needed either of them to trust me. For me, they just had to keep getting the work done.

In our work hanging in with challenging students (and in many stories of this book), the imperative to build trust is never far from the surface. At times, however, trust does not depend on intimacy. Trust has to be seen from the perspective of the student, and we must differentiate our approaches to building that trust as much as we do our strategies for teaching academic subjects. With Jasmine, taking a different approach to trust meant that I did not get what I like most to get from students—a fluid and warm relationship, a bit of gratitude, and a feeling of mutually sharing this time of our lives together.

Jasmine passed my course.

Hanging-In Recommendations and Considerations for Individual Students

1. *Pay attention to the student's capacity to make friends.* Students' relationships with us may mirror the friendships students have with peers, but they are not the same. Support them in making and maintaining friends. Jasmine and Betty had a chance to be friends for life; they truly understood each other's pain and survival strategies. We should always be friendly with students —exuberantly friendly with some and politely friendly with others—but we are not their friends. "Teacher" is a wonderful enough role in their lives.

2. *Repeat instructions in multiple ways and offer previews of lessons.* The capacity to understand and respond to instructions is a variable with challenging students. Many need to hear instructions more than once and see the instructions in writing. They'll do better with previews and alerts given the day before, or even during a few moments at lunch, allowing them to process the words and manage the anxiety that comes from being asked to perform immediately after hearing the details of a task. Support them in asking their peers for clarification if that reduces their anxiety.

3. *Bond with students who require more distance over a shared expectation that they pass the course.* Few challenging students are going to embrace all the goals we have for them; we are seeking academic mastery, and they may be concerned with survival. I wanted Jasmine to love the content of my class as much as I did, but that was not going to happen in my time with her.

4. *Start with what students can do successfully and stretch the expectations.* It is unlikely that they will follow us to the outer edges of their capabilities until they trust us and they trust themselves. Jasmine's success in tolerating her teacher was the biggest life lesson from our class, but that effort kept her from maximizing the academic potential in the course. Don't set up

challenging students for academic failure to prove to them what they might be able to do at their very best.

5. *Stand still; don't experiment every day with a different method.* Comfort, safety, and routine do not mean your lessons will be uninspiring. Give students time to get comfortable with routines. Support them in learning how to work with you, which is best done if you are a predictable provider.

Hanging-In Recommendations and Considerations for the Adult Team

1. *Storytelling:* Share about the student who has challenged you most to keep professional boundaries.

2. *Discuss your understanding of professional boundaries and the variety of ways to work within those boundaries.* Teachers need to be themselves as professionals—students are going to have favorite teachers because of personal preferences. Some teachers will be funnier, some more profound, some more constrained. Working with different types of adults is a necessary skill for living in a diverse society. Teachers need to know what the absolute rules are about sharing personal information, and then they need to enjoy being themselves as professionals.

3. *Review the protocols for working with students who have experienced sexual abuse listed earlier in this chapter.* When staff and students feel safe, the primary curriculum can be at the center of our relationships.

4. *Pool ideas, insights, and information that students have shared about what helps them most.* A student may not communicate with one teacher or school professional but may with another. Ruth shared much useful information about Jasmine, including the wonderful advice to stand still. We are often each other's best resources.

Hanging-In Recommendation and Consideration for Administrators

Establish and disseminate the rules and best practices regarding non-school-based contact with students. Contact through social media can distort and corrupt the professional boundaries many students need for safety. The explosion of social media has altered the traditional norms of what information is available for sharing.

10

Lou

Perfectionism and Ambivalence

We have general guidelines for when children should learn to read, tie their shoes, understand cause and effect, but no child is a textbook case. Challenging students often come to us still developing skills and character traits that are not on a typical timeline. Even when we get to know those students well, the path of their development may remain beyond our comprehension and certainly beyond our control. The story of Lou is a lesson in tolerance for the idiosyncratic ways students grow.

Challenges for Lou:

- Perfectionism
- Uncertainty about gender identification
- Test and performance anxiety

Challenges for her adult team:

- Setting goals for her work
- Being accepting of her struggle with gender identification
- Separating her perfectionism from her thoughtfulness

What's in a Comma?

Lou was staring at her computer screen. We were in a high school language arts class in the computer lab. I always wanted my students to write on computers because then I could demand a higher level of editing and excellence in their work. I wanted them to get through a first draft and then use the power of the software to replace boring adjectives, to adjust the rhythm of phrases, to attend to parallel structure in their verbs, and to delete the unnecessary commas many students sprinkle through their sentences.

Writing time, as I often told students, was also silent time. "No chatting here, folks. You live in a world in which the bells and chimes and noises of all of our devices and machines continually interrupt your thoughts. During writing time, we are creating the space for you to go deeper into your inner world, to find your own thoughts and words. It is a sacred space, and we must be silent to reach it."

Lou sat in our rich silence, pondering a comma near the very end of her first draft. It was a comma that is often known as the Oxford comma, well discussed in Lynne Truss's *Eats, Shoots & Leaves* (2004). It is optional in most cases. I quietly slid a chair next to her. "Can you tell me what's up?" I whispered.

"Would you put a comma here?" she asked. As Lynne Truss would respond, I said, "It depends." I asked her to tell me what she was thinking about. Lou gave me a thorough explanation of the merits of putting in the comma and of leaving it out. She showed me similar places in the text where she had already put in the comma; she wondered if I would care about consistency. She discussed the way the comma could influence how the sentence would be interpreted. "I know no one else would notice, except maybe you, Mr. B. But I would notice. That's what you want, right?"

To myself I silently said, "For you, Lou, that depends." Lou was plagued by her inability to complete her work and hand it in. She had a streak of perfectionism.

Mental health experts have at best a superficial grasp of this character trait; by itself, perfectionism is not recognized as an illness

(Beck, 2012). It's a term commonly attached to certain individuals, but with little available research and practice to suggest exact lines for interventions. We are really hanging in with students on this and doing what we can to help them hang in as well.

The Challenge of Perfectionism

Lou had failed courses throughout her schooling, which was part of the reason she was a year behind in earning her credits toward a diploma. She failed because of her perfectionism and the shadow of depression that trailed closely behind. When her teachers added a small dose of reasonable pressure in the form of tests and deadlines, Lou's production ground to a halt. She would fail again.

Perfectionism lingers at the periphery with many challenging students. Lou's math teacher, Charlotte, saw signs of trouble on the first day of class. Charlotte had given the students a survey to fill out, seeking information about their histories as math students: What had been easy to learn? What had never made sense? What did they hope to learn this year? What did teachers do that helped the most? Lou got stuck on the first question. Charlotte noticed Lou staring straight ahead while her peers were busily writing. When Charlotte quietly suggested that Lou move on to the next question, she declined the offer, at first insisting that with a bit more time she'd give a good answer, then almost immediately contradicting herself by telling Charlotte that the questions were too complex to ever answer accurately. This was the same problem Lou had experienced through the years when she was taking tests. Charlotte wisely told Lou that the survey would be accepted, whether blank or completed. The blank survey communicated a lot of what Lou had struggled with in school through the years. Charlotte had not yet developed a working relationship with Lou, and so backed off from pushing Lou to keep trying. All that Charlotte felt she could do then was communicate that she accepted Lou for who she was that day. That is good advice across the board during the hardest moments with challenging students.

Challenging students may believe that everything about learning comes easily to their more traditional peers. Those peers seem to know their times tables perfectly and the spelling of all the vocabulary words and the formulas for the math problems. These challenging students self-destructively exaggerate the gap between themselves and their peers, which leads them to despair that they could ever bridge it. They do not see a continuum of skills, only that they are flawed and others aren't. They do even less work than they are capable of—often none—because they are sure the work will not be good enough when the teacher picks up her red marker (quick tip—don't use bright red markers that advertise all the errors students make).

Lou had all the information she needed to make a decision about her comma. I told her the decision was up to her, that whatever she decided, her essay would be good enough. I quietly slid away from her. Ten minutes later, when I checked back, she was sitting with the same dilemma.

The challenge of perfectionism can be amplified for many adolescents. Most of them are inventing and reinventing themselves in completely predictable ways. Small decisions, such as the cut of their hair or the color of their cell phone, seem to carry the weight of statements about who they truly are, permanently. Most teenagers weather the storm of adolescence, learning to let go of some concerns, while other concerns (religion, political beliefs, career choices) take root as persistent markers of identity. For Lou, everything she wore and said mattered disproportionately, at least from the view of her parents and teachers. For Lou, the placement of a comma carried the same weight in the moment as her thoughts about who would be her date at the prom.

The Possibility of Being Transgendered

And who would be her prom date was an entirely more complicated concern for Lou than for typical students. Lou was struggling with her gender identity; she wondered if she was transgendered. She had been born with all the external characteristics of a boy. Her parents gave her a boy's name and bought her boy's clothing. Many transgendered people would tell you that they knew they were different from an early age. Not Lou. Her questions about her identity as a boy seemed to come out of the blue when she was in middle school, and they were questions for which she had not yet found answers.

When she started attending a traditional high school, she got her hair cut short, wore jeans and sweatshirt styles common to both boys and girls, and introduced herself as Lou, a name she chose because it was gender neutral. Her teachers did not call her Lou, but instead her legal, unambiguously male name. Many school staff were kind to her; others far from kind. She wrote her name as "Lou" on her papers, and some teachers refused to accept the work or grade it; there was no "Lou" in their record books who could receive credit for the work done. The human being listed in their books with a boy's name began to earn zeroes for grades. Lou soon stopped attending school and was referred to the alternative high school where I worked. She said she was leaning toward identifying herself as a female.

At our school, we had had training and experience with transgendered students. We met with our trainer again shortly before Lou began school. A teacher asked, "Isn't it a big deal to change the name we'll call this student and the pronouns we use? Teenagers are going through so much turmoil already. We don't want to do anything that would contribute to a permanent problem."

The consultant laughed. "Pronouns are not permanent—surgery is permanent! Pronouns are the easy stuff!"

Lou challenged our expectation that she be either a boy or a girl. We were not challenged by students who wondered about various career choices or college plans or where they one day might live. We told them it was normal to be uncertain about such matters and often encouraged them to take their time to make such big decisions, because those decisions would likely determine the course of their future. But we wanted Lou to stop being so uncertain about her gender.

"And don't expect Lou to conform to your notion of what she must be in the end," the consultant said. "Some transgendered people only change their names and pronouns, and they are fine doing that much. Some will receive hormone treatments to change their external appearances. Some will opt for surgery. But there's no rule that says Lou has to reach an end of a continuum of change where *you* might be more comfortable. It's a very personal decision."

Lou privately pondered that very personal decision. She did not announce her gender or her evolving exploration of that gender. We didn't ask other students to publicly declare their gender ("I'm Jeffrey and I'm a boy"), so she was allowed to blend in according to her own wishes. Her teachers were encouraged in some way to privately let Lou know that they were aware of her history and that they would honor her wish to be referred to as "she." I said to her, "I'm your English teacher. My interest is that you are comfortable in class, and when you hand in your work, that you get the commas in the right places, just like everyone else."

So perhaps it was no surprise that weeks later she sat in my class, wondering about all the implications of that one comma, buried near the end of her essay. Lou had made some progress handing in work, and the shadow of her depression had receded. The relentless respectfulness of our staff had made a big difference for her. She had initially been very quiet, as if she couldn't believe that we would not battle her about her gender identification. Even our one-to-one conversations, though critically important, were not enough to remove her doubts about the power of adult authority to damage her fragile sense of self. Her comfort and trust came a day at a time. Her perfectionism was far more a concern to her teachers than her gender. She was not handing in all of her work, some of which we had seen her do correctly.

Some Failure and Some Success with Perfectionism

We had not succeeded with all of our students who suffered from perfectionism. Sometimes perfectionism becomes so extreme it is better described as severe obsessive-compulsive disorder, as was the case with Caroline. On many days, Caroline was unable to complete anything. I watched her start a math worksheet and then vigorously erase her work. I peeked her way as she started the problem again. She seemed to be writing down accurate answers, and then she erased them all. She began again, the same numbers appearing in the same places. She erased them again.

"I have a theory," I said to her quietly. "The numbers are right mathematically, but you want them to be neater, yes?"

When she nodded her reply, I offered to write the numbers for her. I would tell her teacher that I had done the writing, so the imperfect shape of the numbers would not be Caroline's responsibility. "No thanks," she said. "I'll get it." She didn't. Our work with Caroline was ultimately to get her to the right treatment facility and support her family in that transition. We were a safe harbor along her path to a more functional future.

For a similarly distressed student, Simone, we formulated a step-by-step plan. We wanted to protect her from her self-destructive desire to produce flawless penmanship. Specific plans provide observable benchmarks, as well as hope and expectations to make progress. The plan designed for Simone allowed everyone (school staff, Simone, parents) to work as a team, particularly in a situation where clarity and uniformity were essential to protect a student from her worst habits. The plan for Simone included these steps:

1. Simone does all of her writing in school on a computer. She does no written work for homework.
2. Simone does all of her writing in school on a computer. She does one assignment on a computer for homework, which she can do in the school library after school or at home.

3. Simone does all of her writing in school on a computer, except for one task in class per day that she can ask to write with a pencil. She does one assignment on a computer for homework, which she can do in the school library after school or at home.

4. Simone can do half of her writing in school with a pencil. She does one assignment on a computer for homework, which she can do in the school library after school or at home.

5. Simone can choose to write on a computer or with a pencil in school. She can do one task at home with a pencil.

6. Simone can choose to write on a computer or with a pencil in school and for homework.

Because of this student's perfectionism, it was important that no dates or timetables be placed on the plan; she would be able to make academic progress and pass her courses even at step one.

We had some success with Junior, a student who never felt he could write well enough to express his ideas. Words come with many associations—for example, we all have slightly different images when we read, "It was a big book"—and Junior could not control what all readers might imply from his word choices. Written words were imperfect and could never accurately convey what Junior knew he felt inside. He tortured himself over the implications of a single word, and didn't know how to stop his self-editing process. Even with outlines that provided a solid structure for his essays, the meaning of words on paper overwhelmed him. With people, he could talk freely—spoken words seemed less absolute and were tempered by hand gestures and facial expressions, and by the responses he received. He was comforted by the presence of others but could not find a similar comfort in the solitary act of writing. The silence of my writing classes felt to him more like an abyss than a sacred space.

We put Junior on the "writing plan." This plan, which we used for Paul (his story is in Chapter 5), reduces the amount of written work required of the student and provides other choices for demonstrating knowledge. (See Figure 5.2 for a template for the plan.) For example, for his book report, in which the main learning goal was the understanding of character development, Junior drew a map that illustrated a character's life and delivered to his class a wonderful lecture about the roads, alleyways, and rest stops he had drawn, displaying a keen sense of what was important in understanding that character.

For Lou, the first bit of progress came from her math teacher, Charlotte. The survey problem Lou demonstrated on that opening day attuned Charlotte's approach. In her math class of only eight students, Charlotte was able to give Lou very precise praise for her efforts: "Your answer to Problem 7 is right on the mark. I see how you set up the equation using the graph paper and how you drew that little rectangle." As she did from day one with the survey, Charlotte communicated a relentlessly calm acceptance of Lou. That state of calm acceptance was accompanied by Charlotte's hawk eye on every academic task that Lou was able to accomplish. Charlotte slipped in a low-key word of praise here, and a calmly appreciative smile there, lesson after lesson after lesson, day after day after day. In supervision meetings, Charlotte would say, "I am lending her some ego, to see a piece of her work through my eyes, and to agree with me that what I saw was good."

Charlotte could observe so much more about each student and respond so much more meaningfully and precisely because she did not have 30 students in a class, or even 20. The praise was not effusive. She did not tell Lou that she was smart, only that a worksheet was "good enough, and that's all I am asking of you for now." Perfect was the enemy of good.

Charlotte's pedagogy was also a good match for Lou because Charlotte did not give tests. "Let me tell you why I don't give tests," she gently explained to Lou's mother and father on parent night. "I am sitting in a room with only eight students for five hours each week. I am watching your children like a hawk. I talk to each of them every day about their work. I see everything they can do, and I hear each of them tell me their answers to every question. If I needed to give them a test to know what math they were learning, that would mean

I was not paying attention! Sometimes I do give them a quiz so they will know what they can do as well as I know it. And the quizzes give Lou gentle practice with test-taking anxiety. But I don't need to give her a test to know what to teach her next. I've seen that close-up."

Learning Versus Schooling

Hanging in with challenging students can force us to consider what is learning and what is schooling. So many practices common to our notion of what happens in schools are linked to the management of too many young people in too small a space. Teachers are destined to administer tests to gain information on the skills of their students, because they cannot possibly observe and talk to all of their students. When there are too many students in a class to keep track of, teachers must take time from instruction to call out an attendance roll. Lunches are served industrial style. Bathrooms can provide no privacy. All students have to stop a lesson at the same time so other students can take their seats. Semesters end at the same time for every student. Standardized tests are scored by computers. Schools cluster students by ability in the illusion of creating homogeneous instructional groups; even then, it is common practice to pitch instruction to the middle, with teachers hoping to find slivers of time to connect to that outlier student who needs something different. If not, the student fails, and that too is part of schooling.

In the luxury of a small school, Junior's teacher offered him a unique way to present his knowledge of a character, without then having to provide that very same time-intensive opportunity to 125 other students. Lou's teacher Charlotte held her class to high standards without tests, while assembling a rich portfolio of student work. For many challenging students, learning seems to happen when cognitive development is untethered from the institution of large schools. Mainstreaming and "least-restrictive environment" are imperatives for democratic inclusion, but the inevitable practices, limitations, and sheer size of our mainstream schools may never work for a portion of our children.

Unfortunately, many of our students who have been in small schools have worried that their success was not going to hold up in the "real world." I would tease them: "You mean, being consistently kind to you, challenging you in specific ways every day to grow, making plans together, and supporting you as an individual is bad for you?" It is important to tell these students and their families that the most common workplaces in the United States, the ones where most of their children will be employed, are far smaller than a typical public high school (U.S. Census Bureau, 2008). The skills of building relationships, learning and working on teams, communicating, managing conflicts, and setting personal goals—the daily focus of small schools that hang in with our most challenging students—are better preparation for succeeding in the real world than sitting silently through two-hour standardized tests.

Work That Is More Art Than Assignment

Lou still had to make a decision about her comma. The rest of her essay was top-notch. She loved writing. She wanted to be a writer, despite the still occasional plummets into perfectionism. She once tried an extreme technique that had worked with a couple of other students. For 15 minutes she typed with the screen covered, preventing her from the trap of editing and editing and editing each line. Lou did not feel comfortable doing that, but she was a good sport to try it. In retrospect, it wasn't a good idea for her, because writing was her art, not merely a chore to get through. She loved words and phrases, and showed pride in her craft. The rest of her essay was richly written, and her indecision about one comma was as likely a mark of craft as it was a tentacle of obsession. But was it?

"Lou, do you want me to rescue you there?" I asked when I slipped back to her side. "I can make the decision." I took a furtive glance at the clock. Despite all my best intentions to give her the time she needed, I too was habituated to the rules of the game.

"No, Mr. Benson, I can do this. I'm not stuck. Don't worry."

Our work with challenging students requires that we shield them from their worst tendencies until those can be mastered. Sometimes I think the students are like the balls going through a pinball machine, with graduation the result of a successful run through all the obstacles. We shouldn't remove all the bumpers and levers for challenging students because they will need to navigate through life when they graduate, but we can angle the bumpers so they don't crash into them too hard and take away the levers and barriers that are irrelevant to adulthood. School teams need to have significant conversations about what to keep in and what to remove in their curriculum, in their structures, and in their expectations, but I don't think such vital conversations about schooling would filter down to the use of that Oxford comma, sitting at the end of Lou's essay.

"Alright, I'm keeping it," she said. She tapped the keyboard, and then she scanned back through her essay to check on how she had previously handled the Oxford comma. She looked at the clock. "Just in time, huh?" she said, with a bit of humble pride in her voice.

Lou's focus on that comma was healthy and manageable. Her attention was not pathological but generative and artistic. Good work in any field takes time, and we so rarely give students abundant time. Writing can be a chore, but for Lou it was an art, one that often inspired her best pondering and one that could also trigger her perfectionism.

Thomas Hoerr, author of *The Art of School Leadership* (2005), writes about teaching as an artistic achievement, not as a rigid set of behaviors. He wonders how supervising a master teacher might compare to supervising Michelangelo. If teaching should not be reduced to a rigid set of predictable behaviors, neither can the development of a child. My challenge with Lou was one of supervising an emerging artist as much as instructing a typical student with an essay. I was guiding a student who was a budding writer, somewhat perfectionistic, perhaps transgendered, and fully adolescent. I hung in with her by creating a safe place for her to hang in with herself. More than keeping the comma, she was building herself. At least this time it was building. She was still too much in transition for me to ignore her potential to tear her work and herself down.

I would have preferred that Lou had quickly made a decision about that comma. I would have liked her to settle on a gender. I would have preferred that she not see writing as art but simply as a way to finish the assignment. It would have been easier for the rest of us if she conformed to our timetables and our constructs. One of the deep challenges, opportunities, and stresses of working with challenging students is that they force us to look at them as they truly are, in all their ambiguity, within the disequilibrium of what we call schools.

Hanging-In Recommendations and Considerations for Individual Students

1. *Help students manage their worst perfectionistic tendencies,* keeping in mind that the problem may be greater than any single intervention. For some students, it can help to set a time limit after which the teacher will literally take the work out of the student's hands. Set goals that are low level, allowing students to go beyond them if they can but accepting that a low-level accomplishment may be all that she can *finish* right now. Support students in identifying an area in which they want to do their very best, but limit the choice to a task that never has to be completed in order to pass a course or function day to day.

2. *Work closely with the family of a perfectionistic student on setting basic goals.* Keep in close communication and together adjust expectations incrementally.

3. *Provide alternatives to tests.* There are times in our work when we can assess the growth and accomplishments of a student

without high-stakes testing. To do so means we are removing from the curriculum learning how to take tests. As with many challenging students, you cannot achieve every school goal inherent in a task, and surviving a test may not be in a student's current zone of proximal development.

4. *Protect transgendered students from bullying, abuse, and physical attacks.* Discuss with those students times and places in the school that present risks, and help them to navigate, using supports. While it is a goal to make schools safe for everyone, right now they are not, and until that is a norm, our most vulnerable students must receive additional supports.

Hanging-In Recommendations and Considerations for the Adult Team

1. *Storytelling:* Share an example of when you have been able to give a student a lot of time to accomplish a task that others are doing quickly. Have you had students for whom no amount of time is enough as they struggle to make the work perfect?

2. *Discuss ways to protect transgendered students.* Request team professional development to understand and support gay or transgendered students. In many communities, these students are so atypical that their struggles to go to school each day are invisible. They need staff to be their vigorous allies, protecting them so they can learn.

3. *Share observations of skilled students who are not handing in work;* the team may be spotting the outer edges of perfectionism.

4. *Review alternatives to testing as a means of assessing student achievement.* While the investment in time these alternatives require would make them impossible to offer to every student in most traditional schools, the intent is to provide alternatives for those who *need* them.

5. *Develop a list of school structures that can be altered, or even removed, for a given student,* without undermining the school's

sense of community. In Chapter 1, the staff looked at behavioral norms that could be accommodated; here you can look at the procedures and practices that constitute the daily functioning of the school that may actually be optional.

Hanging-In Recommendations and Considerations for Administrators

1. *Nurture a culture of innovation.* School teams won't be able to offer creative alternatives to school practices unless the administration wholeheartedly supports such conversations. Administrators can establish the *process* for approving and implementing atypical accommodations, so that the changes happen in a predictable and collectively understood manner. It is important that staff know they are encouraged to suggest unusual accommodations, because the decision-making process will weed out proposals that are not sustainable.
2. *Directly address the concerns of gay and transgendered students in school initiatives to decrease bullying,* especially in secondary schools.
3. *Provide a single-person bathroom for use by transgendered or gay students;* this is often the bathroom in the nurse's office.
4. *Seek therapeutic services for students suffering from perfectionism.* Survey families to assess the degree of perfectionism that is self-identified in your community.

11

Katerina

Will This Lesson Be Fun?

Every day, teachers face the daunting task of constructing lesson plans that harmonize with how the many different brains in their classrooms learn. Research on brain functioning informs us that there is great diversity and unpredictability in how individuals take in stimulation from the environment, process it, and complete the function we call learning. Add a challenging student or two to the class roster, whose brain functions are obscured by layers of mistrust, disability, boredom, and neglect, and the success of our lesson plans is anything but a safe bet. The story of Katerina is about a student who needs to see the meaning and purpose of each task in order to learn. It is also about the expectation that we will stretch our lesson plans to their limits with the intention of leaving no brain behind.

Challenges for Katerina:
- Lack of trust in schools and teachers
- Rigidly high need to know how each lesson benefits her
- Experience of previous failures that could lead her to fail again
- Verbal quickness adults find disrespectful

Challenges for her adult team:

- Communicating meaning within the prescribed and often disconnected curriculum
- Maintaining a genuine and consistent emotional stance
- Appreciating Katerina's irreverence as intelligence
- Constructing high expectations with her

All the Stolen Minutes

It is midafternoon when the students walk into my classroom. They are worn out from hours of meeting the relentless demands of their teachers. On the board, I have posted the class agenda and my goals for the lesson. Katerina asks, her voice laden with friendly exasperation, "Is this going to be any fun?"

"Oh, I wish it were, my dear Katerina. How about instead that I promise it will be worthwhile, that it will challenge that beautiful mind of yours?"

On a small poster over the board, I keep a line from the poet Richard Brautigan: "My teachers could easily have ridden with Jesse James for all the time they stole from me." It is my mantra, my challenge to myself, my reminder of what is at stake. I will not waste their time. I will not say to them, as is said to them too often, "This is the boring stuff." I do not know whether it is worse to warn them that your lesson is boring and then fulfill that prediction by boring them, or not warn them of the impending boredom and pretend that their boredom is their own fault. But for me, the goal is, in any manner that I can achieve it, that my lesson won't be boring. But will it be fun?

"Katerina, do you ever watch a comedy show on TV? At the end of one of those 30-minute shows, the credits roll. About 75 people have worked on that show, and only sometimes the shows are funny. I am one man alone. Given the odds, you are lucky if you get a single chuckle out of me. You're lucky if I even make you smile." She smiles; I am ahead of the game.

Lifelong Learning

What is important is that my students think, that their beautiful minds are stimulated into activity, that they feel the pleasure of this engagement and its worth, and that it encourages them to live. In the end, the goal of every class is to inspire lifelong learning.

Of course, ideally I want them to master every skill in every curriculum subject area, and I know that we will never fulfill that ideal. Their lives are too chaotic, their histories too imposing. They enter our rooms with jagged profiles of abilities and experiences, with wildly varying access to health care, to nurturance, and to justice. Some of them have not slept enough this week. Some of them were promoted from grade to grade, and now they feel like frauds because they know they didn't learn what the other students learned. They scraped by with a 68 percent average on tests and quizzes and with an ever-growing despair of understanding. Now they are mine, and my goal is to convince them, through the sheer power of their own minds deeply engaged, that they have a lifetime of learning ahead of them, a joyous revelation built within every minute. I am stealing those minutes back from Jesse James.

Betting on My Lesson Plans

I play an imaginary game with myself when I am writing my lesson plans. I imagine a big jar on my desk filled with cash and coins. It is my betting jar. When I am done planning, I picture that jar and I ask myself, "Would I put money in that jar on a bet that this lesson is going to work? Would I bet on myself?" If the answer is "No," as it often is, I have to stay at my desk and keep working. I must be confident in my lesson if I am going to bet on myself. If I have any uncertainty, I feel it in my gut, a visceral warning that I may soon be staring at students who are yet again confused, overwhelmed, frustrated, fantasizing about dropping out, thinking this isn't worth it. My challenging students don't have much tolerance left for any of those feelings.

When I am uncertain in my gut, my next move is to imagine each student going through the activities in my plans, and inevitably I discover the problems. I remember that Diego has just come back to school from a brief hospitalization, and I will need to build in a way for him to catch up, not only with the skills we have been working on but with the reason these skills matter—he'll need time to see how the skills matter to him.

I run my first-period English lesson through the lens of Manuel. He usually has trouble starting essays without an outline, and when he has trouble, his despair infects everyone around him. Manuel uses outlines, not because he is an inferior writer—in fact, he is my most persuasive writer—but because he needs a visual aid to sort through what he believes is important and not important. I have to adjust the plan to leave time for outlining, and I must get to the school office early enough to make copies of the graphic organizers the class will use to jump-start the outlines.

And then there is Katerina, whom I need to assure, as soon as she walks in the math room at the end of the day, that she will be listened to and taken seriously. Katerina is a high-meaning person; she has to connect to the deeper reason behind a lesson to throw herself into it. The reason does not have to be that the lesson will be of immediate practical use. This is fortunate when I am teaching something like the Pythagorean theorem. What would I say?—"I am teaching you the Pythagorean theorem so you can build a stable toolshed." I couldn't possibly fake the usefulness of that—"Katerina, really, you never know when you'll be putting up a toolshed." She would see through any shallow attempts to graft meaning onto a meaningless task. Teachers who try this "you never know" approach lose her respect, and then lose her effort. Dewey spoke of good teachers using "devices of art" to ameliorate the "brutal features" of the curriculum (1938, p. 19). Our high-meaning Katerinas have been with us for a long time.

No, I don't have to invent usefulness, just find a way to intrigue that mind. For Katerina I will say,

> The story about Pythagoras is really interesting. Does anyone know he was a leader of a cult? A mathematical cult? He thought the universe was like a math equation, and if you got your math right, you could think like a god. So what we're going to study today is his most famous math idea, the Pythagorean theorem. Katerina, you have to let me know if understanding this theorem actually makes you feel like you have your hands on the gears of the universe, if you feel like you have the brain of a god. The theorem is an amazing . . .

I sit at my desk, smiling, because I know this will totally hook her; I can see her eyes glistening in anticipation. I have now made adjustments for each of the weaknesses in my plans; finally, I am going to make that imaginary bet in my favor. I am excited to teach my class.

We Count on Students to Be Compliant

All this may sound like an endorsement for "differentiated instruction," for having the right materials, at the right level of challenge, to allow each student to complete the lesson. Schools have improved greatly in such instructional practices; this has been one of the most important changes in schools in the last 20 years. But what is it we are instructing when we differentiate? All the manipulatives and pencil grips on our shelves don't answer that question. Neither do the voluminous pages of mandated content that teachers and students are expected to cover each year. Racing through the requirements, giving minimal attention to the nature of engagement, we count on students to be obedient and compliant. We continue to leave students behind, even students who can do the work, but need to know what for.

All students at various times wonder why we adults ask them to study algebra or the way Steinbeck uses foreshadowing or the atomic weight of lead; most typical students routinely bury that wonder and do what they are told. They know there are predictable social and economic rewards at the end of their education, even if they don't remember most of it, even if they have rarely cared about the worth of what they were asked to do. They have their moments of engagement, their moments of indifference, their moments of sheer boredom. That's school.

For our challenging students, the rewards of completing school can be distant and hazy targets on a far-off horizon. The demands of requirements—"You'll need this to be promoted to the 7th grade"—are as likely to be impediments as they are to be incentives. By high school, and sometimes in middle school, students have spent most of their capital set aside for boredom and disconnection. In *The Power of Their Ideas*, Deborah Meier explains their dilemma:

> [T]o put up with twelve years of serious high-stakes study young people have to want to be there. . . . They need a bridge that connects their understanding of the meanings of the world to the ones being offered by "capital E Education." That's assuming Education is something worth crossing the boundary to get!" (1995, p. 163)

Making learning worthwhile in the moment is a crucial issue for hanging in with our challenging students. They need lessons that have some value for them today, and then tomorrow, and then the day after that. Or we leave them behind, and we have already left behind way too many. High school graduation rates are less than 70 percent in many states (National Center for Higher Education Management Systems, 2012); nationally, the rates have been static since the imposition of requirements to pass standardized tests. Telling them they have to know something for the test is not enough.

When a Student Doesn't Start Working

We can use all the minutiae of our mandated curriculum as grist for the mill of the much larger enterprise of becoming lifelong learners. To do so, don't invent wildly unlikely scenarios to defend the importance of every fragment of required content. Don't hide behind some unknown "they" who are requiring this content be taught. Our students who are marginally hanging on, but so filled with potential, will pull even further away. I can see Katerina now, slouching deeper into her seat, peering out the window, feeling the pull of the streets.

Even your best lesson plan may not capture the engagement of a student who is struggling to find a reason to do the work. Here are some approaches that may open the pathway for that student on a given day. They are all intended to avoid a power struggle and ultimatums; instead they build, and build upon, a relationship of trust. These approaches express an expectation that the student can find success and worth in making the effort, and they can be used to appeal to the quirks of interest in each individual.

Approaches based on a student's knowledge and skills:

- You have a strength in this lesson: ____
- You have information we need: ____
- You will find this part a challenge worthy of your intelligence: ____
- This task has absolutely no daily life application. It is totally about working through the challenge of it. For you, it will help you get better at hanging in with a tough task.
- If you get good at this task, you will probably do these other tasks better as well: ____
- Here's the part I think will be easy ____, and here's the part I think will be challenging ____.
- Show me how to set it up and talk me through it. That'll be good enough for now.
- I bet you can find all the information you are going to need even if you get stuck on what to do with it.

Approaches based on a student's creativity:

- You can probably do this in an interesting way: ____
- You can probably do this at a higher level: ____
- There are three different options for approaching this task. You have to find the one that makes sense to you.

- I have no idea whether you will find this worthwhile, but I think it has possibilities.
- What do you think you need to do next? What are some things that might work?

Approaches based on a student's relationships:

- You can work one to one with another student.
- You have a specific part of this to do for the group. ____
- I need your feedback on this lesson. Is there anything you do like about it?
- I love this stuff—here's why: ____
- This is a lot like this other thing you do, ____, but not exactly the same. Give it a shot and let me know ____.
- Do you want five minutes to just chill out? I can give you that.

No Child Will Be Left Out of the Plans

Every student, no matter what the challenge, is entitled to a lesson plan that can work. Rather than testing and finger-pointing, No Child Left Behind could have meant that no child will be left out of the plans. Tests come way later. The first issue is sparking every mind—"Katerina, this math lesson is going to push you to figure out how to make a graph without being given the scale!" To reach that ideal, teachers need to have relationships with these most challenging students. I knew Katerina would be intrigued by setting up the scale of a graph, even though she may never in the rest of her life outside of school be compelled to make such a graph. What she will be compelled to do, and what I will compel her to do, is to engage.

To set the hooks of interest and purpose, teachers need information that reveals the complexity of their most challenging students. They need training, limited class size, and the biggest resource of all: time. Teachers need time to build relationships with their most challenging students, time to confer with other staff, and time to stick with a lesson plan until it is massaged into shape for every student walking through the door. Teachers need time to plan for the lifelong learning potential buried in their most challenging students.

Katerina doesn't need this speech. What she needs from me is a sense of purpose, a commitment to not waste her time. She has to know that every day I will remember to be in her corner, to help her make sense of this chaotic world. She and I have had enough great classes together, enough heart-to-heart talks, enough times pondering the most elegant solution to a problem using the Pythagorean theorem —"Katerina, look at that again. You missed a way to cut all that work in half!"—for her to trust me.

"Is this going to be any fun?" she asks.

I say to her, "All I can tell you is that I think you will be glad your mind got its exercise. That's the plan."

"I'll let you know about that," she promises, or warns, me. And she smiles. I am now two steps ahead.

Hanging-In Recommendations and Considerations for Individual Students

1. *Help each challenging student find the moments in the assignments that speak to his or her quirky way of thinking*—"Katerina, when you get to Question 3, I bet you will have so much to say." "Diego, there's a way of doing this task that uses graphs that you are particularly good at." Within each lesson's tasks are opportunities that foster and acknowledge individualized thinking. Challenging students need to find and refind their identity as thinkers in the work we ask them to do. Use the list of approaches given earlier in the chapter to help students find a reason to begin a task.

2. *Find delight in students who ask "Why?" and honestly answer the question from their perspective.* High-meaning students like Katerina, who ask "Why are we doing this?" are often met with curt responses. Their questions can seem disrespectful, but responding with "I am glad you asked that question" creates an opening to learn what the student needs in order to do the

work well. Acknowledgment that the question is a good one—and shouldn't it be?—creates a pathway to a relationship. In lesson plans, consider the "why" questions from the point of view of your most challenging student.

Hanging-In Recommendations and Considerations for the Adult Team

1. *Storytelling:* Share a time when one of your challenging students was engaged in her or his work. What was your mixture of content and processes that sparked thinking and engagement?
2. *Provide time and resources when a challenging student finds a connection.* For many challenging students who seek a meaningful experience in school, the teaching team can follow the students' surprising moments of engagement. For these students, rekindling the joy of learning so often comes from being given the time and support to grab onto one curriculum strand. Teachers need flexibility to build on student interest. A single lunch period or study period set aside for a conversation with a student can alter the path of a student's lifetime engagement. Teachers can provide impromptu coverage for each other when those potentially magical opportunities arise. Everyone may benefit in the long run.

Hanging-In Recommendations and Considerations for Administrators

1. *Develop lesson plan templates that ask for more than listing the required standard addressed in the lesson.* The lesson plan should identify the value of the content from the student perspective. To prompt teachers to identify how the lesson will lead challenging students to engage, the template should ask "What action is *the student* expected to do?" and "What is the hook?"

2. *Provide teachers with summaries of IEPs*, particularly highlighting the most significant accommodations for each student. See Figure 6.1 for an IEP summary template.

3. *Fight for maintaining arts and music programs, in any form possible.* Challenging students need schools to provide abundant opportunities to find their inner passions. If budgets for those departments are cut, seek community resources to bring these important opportunities to school (interns from local colleges; visiting artists).

12

Derek

Slow Processing

Schools are hectic places, jam-packed with people and requirements, schedules and high-stakes testing. Prescriptions for educational reform often press for longer days but rarely in the interest of rushing less. Schools are increasingly fast-paced, but challenging students, particularly those with processing deficits, need us to slow down, not to hurry them, or layer on a second or third demand when they are still struggling to meet the first. Time may be the most valuable resource of all if we plan to leave no child behind—time for moments of patience, reflection, and connection. The story of Derek illustrates how a student can silently struggle with a disability that is mistaken for defiance and how time can be an essential accommodation.

Challenges for Derek:

- Slow language processing
- Unsuccessful academic history
- Many experiences of conflict with school authorities
- Depression
- Lack of goals

Challenges for his adult team:

- Finding patience repeatedly
- Balancing commitments to protocols with commitments to individual students
- Establishing high expectations with considerable scaffolding
- Recognizing our countertransference
- Working with latent student strengths

All That He Meant to Say

Derek would tell you that he was suspended all those times at his old school for "stupid things." He didn't say much more than that. He didn't suppress a chuckle when he said it. He didn't seem proud. Maybe angry. One time when I spoke to Derek (it was so rarely *with* him) he said, "That teacher didn't have to suspend me. Just because I walked away from him."

"What was going on? What did the teacher want?"

"It was stupid. He wanted me to take off my hat. So I was going to my locker to put it away."

"Derek, did you tell him where you were going? Or did you just walk away from him without saying anything?"

Derek stared at me and then past me, over my shoulder, down the long empty hallway. I waited 30 seconds in silence. "Alright," I said, "thanks for letting me know what happened. You better get going to class."

I had never met a student who processed language as slowly as Derek did. Reports from teachers throughout his school career were consistent on that observation. The little writing he produced for required tests and essays was always subsequently marked up with directives to "Expand on this" or "Provide more details." He would rarely explain his thinking, even when gently cajoled to do so. "I just told you what I was thinking," he would answer. It took a long time of hanging in with Derek to appreciate that he was being honest. The words he had said conveyed all that he meant to say. Any demand that the adults would make to tell us more—from our perspective, an invitation that conveyed our deepest desire to understand—was seen from his perspective as another instance in which he was simply not being understood.

A Quiet Way to Be Miserable in School

We live in a post-Freudian world. Were you to say, "My brother is paranoid," most people would have a notion of how your brother behaved. Were you to say, "My brother has a receptive auditory disability," most people would be confused. It is common for school personnel to attribute students' behaviors to their attitudes, their personalities, their family. It is less likely that we will consider learning styles and disabilities as primary factors in a challenging student's behavior. Many students with a variety of learning difficulties develop an emotional layer of resistance, which serves as a protection against the hour-to-hour cognitive difficulties they have faced through the years. The paperwork on Derek noted his slow processing speed, after a richer description of his uncooperative behaviors.

For Derek, it was easier to say "The school was stupid" than "I have always struggled to be understood." Referencing the attitude to a similar disability, Ned Hallowell (2012) writes: "ADHD is NOT a disease of the will, nor a moral failing. It is NOT caused by a weakness in character, nor by a failure to mature. Its cure is not to be found in the power of the will, nor in punishment, nor in sacrifice, nor in pain." Being slow to process language is one of the quietest ways to be miserable in school. Derek's adolescent protection from all the moral judgments he had absorbed—hat pulled low over his eyes, blank reactions to school instructions, minimal acknowledgment of adult outreach—certainly made him seem a threat to the welfare of his community.

Derek's emergence into adolescence complicated every analysis of his behavior. His conflicts with high school staff were not atypical for many a well-adjusted teenager, pushing out against the rules that make schools flow smoothly for most of its citizens. His language processing delays were likely hardwired into his brain functioning, but his parents reported that he could chat with his friends at a local music store: "You should hear him talk about guitars. He's building one at home. It's taking him forever, but who cares? He goes online to buy parts. He gets ideas from the guys in the store. He smiles when he is there." Derek satisfied many of the conditions that would lead to a diagnosis of depression, but that might have been situational, unique to school, or even parts of school. Observing him sitting with his peers at lunch would lead to a different conclusion than seeing him in classes. He was not the chattiest person with his peers, but he smiled and occasionally inserted a story of his own into the free-flowing teenage narrative.

Schools had not been a good match for developing the best potential in Derek. Traditionally, we ask students to respond to us far too quickly and verbally: "The average wait time after asking a question before the teacher jumps in with cuing, redirection, telling the answer, or restating the question is 0.5 seconds" (Saphier & Gower, 1997, p. 309). Derek couldn't produce a response worthy of his thinking in less than one second, or even five. The few words Derek would say had to carry a tremendous amount of meaning, because there would not be abundant time allocated for him to support and reexplain himself with a lot of other words. The speed of adults, coupled with adult authority and expectations, often shut him down completely. He learned to withdraw both behaviorally and cognitively; teachers did not hang in with him and support him to expose the layers of his thoughts and emotions. He learned that his way of being would often not be tolerated (Siegel, 1999). So he walked away to store his hat in his locker without another word said. What's the problem with that? Actually, he knew what the problem was, in terms of the consequences the adults meted out. The consequences, unfortunately, did not teach Derek to be more careful but to care even less.

Bedrock Concerns: Security, Belonging, Recognition, Control

Working with Derek, especially when he was struggling, required us to go to the deepest repository of patience we could find in our professional toolkit. I came across him one day as he was being sent from his class because he was refusing to do work. I volunteered to walk with him to the chairs outside the guidance department, where students would be expected to talk with a counselor. I just wanted to get Derek to that place. He stood in the hall, unmoved by my "C'mon, Derek" and my step toward our destination. "Will you walk with me?" I asked.

"Why?" he responded flatly. He stared past me.

This was a situation Derek had coconstructed with schools and teachers for years. Adults could not know if Derek was being provocative. Maybe Derek was throwing out a verbal rope to engage me in a tug of war; maybe he would keep asking "Why?" after every explanation just to observe the adult become frustrated. It didn't seem possible that he was ignorant of basic school rules and procedures. Perhaps his "why" was an honest and unanswerable expression of his decade-long disengagement from the standard business of schools. My best guess was that "[u]nderneath it all [were] feelings of incompetence, a fear of being overwhelmed by life's demands, and a feeling of being unable to meet other people's standards" (Taylor, 2001, p. 50). I could remind him of—really, threaten him with—the progressive consequences he would face for his refusal to follow school rules: detention; call home; suspension.

None of those consequences would have made a difference. I knew that eventually he would walk away from that spot; he was a teenager—he had to eat. The challenge was for Derek to move of his own free will, to not create further distance between himself and the community. In their groundbreaking work on conflict resolution, *Getting to Yes*, Fisher, Ury, and Patton (1991) urge us to examine the "bedrock concerns which motivate all people" (p. 48), including security, a sense of belonging, recognition, and control over one's life, none of which Derek had ever fully felt in his school experiences. In that moment with Derek, the list of his probable concerns paralleled those I was juggling: Derek's emotional development; my relationship with him; his relationship with the school community; the need for a safe school, which is created, in part, by its rules and rituals. I could say, "Derek, if you don't walk with me to the guidance department, you will be suspended." It had happened before, and I just had to say those words, and it would likely happen again. He wasn't moving.

Was reinforcing the school discipline code the most important interest I needed to attend to in that moment? No one was looking at us in the hall. There would be no contagion if I took a slower route. I could keep the threat of suspension in my toolkit for now.

How to Make Temporary Exceptions

The term "bureaucratic ritualism" describes when organizations value the consistency of enforcing rules over the impact of a rule on a given individual. One of the joys and challenges of individualizing education is to pull a child out of the common practice. Staff should consider three criteria for making temporary exceptions to rules as we hang in with challenging students:

1. *Is it in the best interest of the individual?* The most obvious argument for using the discipline system is that "Derek has to learn to follow rules." Absolutely. For some students, the lack of organizational consistency can be confusing; following the rules can be the most *compassionate* action we can take. That was not the case with Derek. It was in the best interest of Derek to learn to explain himself. He had to learn to know which adults he could trust. He had to learn to follow rules because they made sense, for him and for the world. He had to learn, through our examples, to have compassion. He had to learn that I also had a job to do that limited my options. John Dewey (1938) wrote, "The belief that all genuine education comes

about through experience does not mean that all experiences are genuinely or equally educative" (p. 25). Hanging in with challenging students means we must consciously choose the lesson that is most teachable and worthwhile in the moment. In that moment, I liked the prospects for learning all the other lessons more than the lesson about instantly following rules.

2. *Do we have the resources to carry out a different plan?* In this situation, the resource I needed to allocate to Derek was my time. I was heading to my office to tackle the endless piles of papers that always sat there. I was not keeping someone else waiting. Schools tend to be fast-paced environments, in which adults rarely set aside the time to fully listen. In addition to all the feelings provoked by student noncompliance, we chafe at allocating the precious resource of time to manage yet another problem. Students like Derek do not bring out the best in teachers who are stressed. He was a lightning rod for countertransference. I was not in a rush, so I could offer a time-consuming alternative to instantaneous disciplinary action.

3. *Can the plan be done safely within the community?* "What if everyone wanted to do that? All hell would break loose!" is a common response when we make an exception. It is critical to know when a predictable consequence is the symptom of bureaucratic ritualism or when the predictable consequence is necessary for the individual and for the community. Derek wasn't going to advertise that he had defied a teacher request and gotten away with it. Derek was not a role model who would influence others to repeat this behavior. He had not done a behavior so egregious that a clear, consistent, and unequivocal adult response was needed to underscore our commitment to the safety of the community. He could be dealt with as a frustrated, confused, overwhelmed individual, with no impact on the safety of the community.

"Well, what do you want to do now, Derek? At some point in this we have to end up at the guidance department—that's not an option.

It's how the school is set up. But I am not in a rush. What do you want to do *now*?" I leaned against the wall of lockers to underscore that I was going to give him time to think.

In many situations in this book, challenging students force school staff to prioritize on the spot the lessons we most want to teach (see the story of Jay in Chapter 8). I did not want Derek to think that society will bend its rules for him if he is just stubborn enough. I also did not want him to think that society had so little compassion for the plight of a struggling young man, whose worst infraction was taking up our valuable time. I wanted Derek to believe that there was room for someone like him, if he would come halfway. I did not know whether he was digging in his heels for a fight, whether he was emotionally frozen in place, or whether he needed time to think through his options.

In reflecting on his own struggle to be compassionate with an individual and consistent with rules, Peter Elbow (1986) writes, "We have an obligation to students but we also have an obligation to society. . . . Our loyalty to students asks us to be their allies and hosts as we instruct and share. . . . Our commitment to society asks us to be guardians or bouncers" (p. 142). Elbow advocates that we embrace both the rules and the student, that we wholeheartedly allow ourselves to alternate between those contrary loyalties, and that we not compromise on either loyalty. Working with challenging students demands that we embrace as many loyalties as we can. I was not ambivalent about the school protocol to go to the guidance department; it was a useful function, and Derek would not be harmed by it. Bureaucratic ritualism would ask me to have no other loyalty than enforcing our rule at standard school speed.

"I want some water," Derek said. The fountain was in the opposite direction from the guidance department. He would have to pass a number of classroom doors along the way and then pass them again on his way back.

"Go ahead. I'll wait here for you."

He walked very slowly down the hall. At one point he stopped. Was he testing me? Had he forgotten that I was waiting for him? Did he think of something so puzzling that he had to stand still to think it through? I resisted calling out to him to hurry up, and a few seconds later he continued his slow trek. He stood in front of the fountain many moments before he took his drink, and then again after he was done with the water. He slowly walked back toward me.

The Complicated Option of Accommodating

I had accommodated Derek with no guarantee that he would then comply with the protocol to walk with me to the guidance area. There are no guarantees when we accommodate; unfortunately, we often expect an implicit quid pro quo. Many of us have, when faced with a class of students protesting the homework requirement, said, "OK, instead of all the problems on the page, just do the odd numbered ones," and the next day when the students behave in their typically rowdy fashion, we have said resentfully, "Look at how you are behaving, and after I allowed you to do only half the assigned homework!" But the students had never agreed to change their behavior because we altered the homework task; that was an unspoken condition of ours. When we accommodate students, we have to be very aware, if we have not made it a shared plan, that the accommodation is our decision, an option we have chosen from our toolkit. Derek had walked off to get water, with no agreement about how long he would take to do it, nor whether he would then follow me down the hall to the guidance department. I had accommodated in hopes that my gesture would develop trust, the prerequisite for a working relationship. Taking small risks to build trust with students who have depleted to almost nothing their trust in the institution of school is a necessity of hanging in.

"Derek," I said quietly when he finally returned, "I have to get back to my office. Nothing personal, I just have work to do now. And I have to finish my responsibility of seeing you to the guidance department. You don't have to say anything. I am going to walk there. I will tell them you are on your way. When I see you are in that part of the hallway, I will leave. I don't have to stand there until you are in a chair—I just have to know you are going to get there. So, I am going to start walking there now."

I walked much more slowly that I usually do. I arrived at the guidance department well before he turned the hallway corner and came into view. As I passed him on the way to my office I said, "Thanks. I appreciate this."

The Two-Way Street of Building Trust

There were many opportunities with Derek to build trust, as there are with every challenging student. We adults have to take lots of small risks and get as much from them as we can. It was Derek's responsibility to earn my trust; I could not put that in place for him, only give him the chance to cocreate a relationship (Taylor, 2001). When hanging in with a student and using opportunities to build trust, these guidelines can be helpful:

1. *Keep the risk small, so the learning and relationship building is not overwhelmed by what the student may or may not do.* In this story, Derek was taking up my time and nothing more.
2. *Be aware of the accommodations you are making because you are deciding to make them.* The student has not forced you to make the accommodations. Derek asked for water, and it was my decision to say yes. I could have said no.
3. *If the student fulfills the expectation, let the volume of your praise match the action.* Derek did not need an effusive lecture from me about how his life will be enhanced by the walk to the water fountain and back. A simple and sincere thanks was as much as he knew he deserved. Sincerity builds trust.
4. *If the student fails to follow through, keep the lecture brief about the disappointment you feel.* Adjust your expectations for next time to a smaller step but make sure there is a next time.

Derek did not generalize his trust. The pains and scars he carried from so many years of conflicts did not get healed in any epiphany. Each school adult had to build a relationship with Derek step by step. In his mind, each moment of trust was an exception to the rule, and each adult who gave him opportunities to build trust was an exception, too. At staff meetings, we shared stories about those precious moments with Derek. There was the day in art class when his offer to help another student with a perspective drawing was accepted. There was the time his English teacher asked him for his critique of a movie, and he slowly gave a rich analysis of the physics of how cars were driven in a crash scene. I gave him an extra 10 minutes to get to class, with no penalty, when he and his girlfriend had a big conflict. I was impressed that he intended to go to class at all, and he did, the full 10 minutes late.

Derek slowly gave us the benefit of the doubt, and we did the same for him, but we had to take the first risk on that path. He graduated, an outcome that had never been a foregone conclusion. On graduation night, after his girlfriend gave me a big hug, he initiated a brief hug with me as well. He shook hands with some staff, hugged a few others, too. We were most pleased that he was accepted into, and planned on attending, an auto mechanics school. More school for Derek, an amazing choice.

Hanging-In Recommendations and Considerations for Individual Students

1. *Let students know when you are making an accommodation for them.* I am distinguishing these from the mandated accommodations on an individualized education plan (IEP). Be explicit: "I am going to let you do that this time—I may never let you do it again." Many students will ask for an accommodation that can sound like a manipulation, so make sure that accommodation will meet an interest of yours.

2. *Tell the student how much time you have to be with him for a task.* Ask the student how much time he thinks he needs. Help him develop a sense of his own pace. "Derek, how's five minutes sound for that? I will check back with you then."

3. *Seek quality of work over quantity.* Derek could write a good paragraph in the time it took his peers to write a page. His paragraph was expected to be top-notch.

4. *Find the edge of trust with each student.* Just as we choose books for a student based on our assessment of reading ability, be judicious in the opportunities you choose to build trust. Remember, you are not only developing your relationship with a student whose deepest interest to be recognized is at stake, but perhaps more importantly, you are letting the student experience his own ability to be trustworthy, a secondary curriculum goal. "Derek, before I let you go to do that, I want you to think for a moment: will you be able to keep your word on this? I will remember what happens here. Don't go if you think you may not be able to do what you say."

5. *Stand firm with rules* and *help the student find a way to comply.* It can take time for a student who has a long history of pain and frustration to weather the storm of feelings that have to subside before he can be compliant. Sometimes it just takes time, with no need to have the student explain everything.

Hanging-In Recommendations and Considerations for the Adult Team

1. *Storytelling:* Share when have you been very creative in developing a trusting relationship with a student. When have you struggled with the dual loyalty to both student and institution that can sometimes be in conflict? What does your story tell us about managing that conflict?

2. *Brainstorm ways to build trust in the natural ebb and flow of the school day.*

3. *Identify students who are diagnosed with processing-speed deficits.* Throughout this book, students with various disabilities and challenges have strengths, often nonverbal strengths, that are not apparent in the busy environment of school. They will likely feel better able to tackle your academic tasks if you let them know that it is okay to work slowly, and also when you provide them with opportunities to show you what they can do well.

4. *Provide time frames to check back on progress.* Even as uncommunicative a student as Derek could predict how much work he might produce in a given time. The teaching team can scaffold student self-awareness, relationship building, and exertion of effort by setting mutually agreed upon work targets for 10-minute intervals. The team can let the students know they will accept the good work the students produce in that time. To start with, aim to establish a baseline of competency; you can ramp up the work expectation after that.

5. *Establish with the teaching team a minimal number of rules that demand instant compliance.* As discussed in Chapter 1, teaching teams do well to organize expectations into absolutes, areas to ignore, and teachable moments. It is rare that we have to teach speed. Protocols for the adults protect us from the anger and frustration (countertransference) almost all of us feel when a student is not quickly doing what we are asking, or telling, them to do. If everyone on the team has agreed to slow down, it will be easier for you do the same.

Hanging-In Recommendation and Consideration for Administrators

Develop a protocol to slow down the escalation to suspension. While some behaviors warrant immediate and temporary removal from the community (often when the interest of safety is primary), many incidents between staff and students are step-by-step escalations.

In one school, the protocol is that the staff person who started the interaction with the student could not be the staff person who suspended the student: "Derek, I am going to get someone else to be with you who might be more helpful now."

13

Leah

The Total School Environment

Differentiating curriculum is now a common expectation in schools, allowing students with differing learning styles to work together in the same room. Students who present many complex challenges often need a differentiated *school*, where the potential in every element of the environment and curriculum is considered for its effect on student success. Within this attention to detail also lies one last lesson—the importance of how we say good-bye. Leah's story is about a student's struggle with loss and addiction. It's also about a school's commitment to support its students through all their transitions, which is its richest curriculum.

Challenges for Leah:

- Substance abuse
- Difficulty asking for help
- Trauma and depression
- Violence in the community

Challenges for her adult team:

- Establishing a consistently supportive school environment

- Working as a team
- Identifying our countertransference
- Respecting privacy and maintaining community

Immortal No Longer

When I was studying to become a teacher, one of the common beliefs about adolescents was that they thought they could get away with dangerous behavior and emerge unscathed. They could drive fast, smoke and drink, stay out late, and venture into the rain and snow without a coat. Our adult warnings fell on deaf ears. Adolescents saw themselves as another species, bursting with the possibilities of life, practically immortal in their capacity to bounce back again and again from what adults saw as foolish risk-taking behavior. During my internship in an inner-city school in the 1970s, a speaker at an assembly told the students that, according to statistics, one of them would die in a car accident before graduation. All the students turned their heads, scanning the crowd to guess who that unlucky victim of fate might be—it was certainly going to be somebody else.

Thirty years later, when Leah enrolled in our small high school, that patina of immortality had been worn away for a subset of her generation. Leah knew a lot of teenagers who had died. They had died from drug overdoses, suicide, acts of random violence, and gang killings. As Geoffrey Canada (1995) so powerfully described in *Fist, Stick, Knife, Gun*, the influx of crack cocaine and handguns into many neighborhoods upended completely the social order of those communities. Many students now came to our schools worried that they would not live to be adults, even those who grew up in relatively safe neighborhoods. Some students were worried because they did not think they could be protected from all the violence around them; others because they had already accepted that they would lead a life of violence. Many peers had dramatically left them forever without a chance to say good-bye.

Leah coped with her fear by smoking marijuana. Trauma expert Judith Herman notes, "Adaptation to [a] climate of constant danger requires a state of constant alertness" (Cole et al., 2005, p. 16). Constant alertness is exhausting. Leah said that her drug use allowed her to relax and to fall asleep at the end of each day. Those day-to-day imperatives of maintaining fearful watchfulness and finding relief from that anxiety took precedence over her schoolwork. Leah was not a strong student in the standard curriculum. For her to succeed, she would have to exhibit the determination of what we called a "plugger."

Pluggers Take Care of Themselves

A plugger was a middle-of-the-pack student who dedicated herself to studying, asking for extra help, and using all of her inner resources to block out distractions and laboriously complete her assignments. We had seen many pluggers make it through to graduation, perhaps more pluggers than students for whom academics were less difficult. When pluggers found their ability to do the work, they were a pleasure to have in class—you knew someone was always listening and someone would always do the homework. Our teachers playfully fought over having the pluggers assigned to their class rosters. Conversely, pluggers could be disdainful of their peers who were struggling. The effort the pluggers had put into taming their inner demons, and then the effort they exerted to pay close attention, limited their compassion for those who had yet to find their pathways to success. Pluggers took care of themselves.

Leah's substance abuse prevented her from being a plugger. It prevented her from doing many things. She came to school late, sometimes with her homework, often looking as if she had barely woken up. She was quietly apologetic and self-loathing. She was the type of student who broke our hearts because she didn't blame her teachers for her own feelings of frustration and failure, but turned those feelings on herself. "It's not your fault, Mr. Benson," she would say to me in our English class, fighting to stay awake, her eyes rimmed with dark circles, her work a messy scrawl. "You're just doing your job."

"That's right," Martin added. Martin was funny, very friendly, and a chronic avoider of hard work. "Mr. B., we all really appreciate that you show up every day with these cool lessons and your positive attitude. We appreciate that you are doing your job. Of course, it doesn't mean we'll do the work." Leah smiled slightly, more embarrassed by her failures than Martin was by his.

We Control So Much, but Not the Students

Martin's comment touched on a sobering aspect of our work. When we are hanging in with challenging students, we come to realize what we do and don't have control over. As the school staff, we ultimately controlled the requirements, the curriculum, the schedule, the discipline system, the lesson plans, the type of furniture in rooms, the lunchtime procedures, the length of the school day, the access to our offices, the tolerance for public displays of affection, the location of the pencil sharpeners. We thought deeply about each of these elements of the school, and often there were conflicts among staff in making these decisions (perhaps with the exception of the location of pencil sharpeners) because we cared so much to get the total environment right, and because there was one aspect of the environment we did not control: the students.

Acknowledging how little we control the students we are supposed to be controlling is a sobering and necessary realization, a daily understanding that highlights the difference between working in the mainstream and working primarily with our challenging students. There are days that challenging students walk into class and are not ready to function as learners. Balancing the attention we give to those struggling students and the attention we give to their peers is hard work. The rituals and structures in the environment that we control are a form of caring for them all.

In the mainstream, we also care about each student. We differentiate lessons as required by individualized education plans (IEPs), and our success each day is directly correlated to how many of the planned objectives we cover. The core curriculum of academic objectives is a long journey, a railway track of requirements that can be best rolled over by a steadily moving train of lessons, one after the other, rolling at a brisk pace down the tracks from September to June. There's not much leeway to slow down, especially with the high-stakes tests looming on the horizon. Students who fall off the train have to run to catch up. It is primarily an objective-by-objective-driven operation, by design a train filled with model student passengers.

Hanging in with challenging students means you plan Tuesday's lesson after you see how far you got on Monday, given the real students sitting in front of you. I always knew the trajectory of my curriculum, but there was no guarantee that the students who overcame all their struggles to make it through the door each day would be ready to run with me. Some days we walked. Some days we crawled forward. Some days we flew ahead, and it was exhilarating. My goal was to make them mentally "sweat" as much as I could each day, to push them as far as I could, and to know when their capacity to stay on task was breaking down.

The staff's main job was to renew the school's culture and environment each day, re-creating what was in our control. Through our rituals, structures, and relationships, the environment allowed me to provoke as much progress as I could for whoever arrived at the classroom door. I was always thrilled when Leah arrived at the door—not satisfied that arriving was enough, but it certainly was a prerequisite to any progress. "Leah, you are here. Fabulous. Let's see what you can do today."

Teach the Students Sitting in Front of You

The teachers I supervised were not evaluated on how many of the objectives they covered each semester. Who could predict what the students would be able to accomplish as they pushed up against their fears, as they took two steps forward and one step back on the road to stability? The teachers were evaluated on how they attuned Tuesday's lesson plans to the work of Monday's class, the work of the real students who sat in front of them. The direction of the curriculum was clear, the acceleration determined day to day.

The teachers used their supervision time with me, and their time with the rest of their adult teams, to hone in on each student: "Is Edgar doing homework in your class?" "I think Lisa is coasting a bit, so I am going to push her to expand on her writing." "Brittany is on a roll. I am assigning her extra short stories, and she wants to talk to her guidance counselor about adding a foreign language course." "My class did really poorly on a quiz this morning—can you look it over and tell me what you think?" "Leah isn't doing well."

I held high expectations for Leah and my other students. We were reading *The Old Man and the Sea*, as part of a unit that explored the power of writing to inspire through the students' identification with characters who faced a challenge. A teacher friend of mine was also using that book, in a high-performing mainstream school. We planned a similar start to the unit: in our respective classes, students would analyze how Hemingway used details to build the character of the old man. My friend and I were each going to give a brief introduction to the book, have our students read silently the first two pages, and then have them choose from a series of prompts to write a one-paragraph analysis. We both would write the prompts on the board in our classrooms ahead of time and get the students working as soon as they settled into their seats.

His lesson plan covered one day; mine covered two. My students did not routinely settle into their seats, even with our friendly rituals and my predictable requests. I set aside a couple of minutes in my plan to greet each student personally, to rekindle the connection with me that they still often needed in order to follow my expectations that they take academic risks. When I gave them their copies of *The Old Man and the Sea*, I asked them where they planned to keep the book when they left class, because I wanted them to bring it back the next day. For many of them, keeping their materials in order was a work in progress. I asked them to talk a little about the last book they had finished and how they had dealt with the times when they got bored and wanted to put it aside. Because they were not a group that generally read for pleasure, I took them through some prereading routines, looking at the cover art, the blurbs, the size of the font, and the number of pages (they were impressed that such a famous book could be so short).

I gave them a dramatic review of Hemingway's life. I told them a little about how the first few pages would unfold, so that they weren't diving blindly into the text, even this text that was so easy to decode. They were fluent enough readers and filled with things to say, but their student habits were inconsistent. I drew their attention to the prompts on the board for their essay, giving each prompt a thorough explanation. I also reviewed a list of the elements of a good paragraph—they were expected to meet every standard of good writing. "OK, I think you are ready to start this great book."

With all of that activity, including their many questions, stories, and tangential commentary, 40 minutes were well used. My friend did not individually greet each student (he had 26 of them), did not have them organize their backpacks to make a place for the book, did not predict difficulties, and did not spend any time with the cover and blurbs. He expected the students to read the writing prompts on their own when they were finished with the silent reading (he would be available to answer individual questions), and he told them he expected a "solid paragraph" without needing to explicate what that meant (again, he would later on give individual attention to some students as the need arose).

In this fashion, every day, he raced along the tracks of his mandated curricula objectives at twice the speed of my class. In the end, my students would gain just as much as his students from the text, would answer many of the same high-level questions, and would produce very well-edited writing. After *The Old Man and the Sea*, his class had time to read *The Grapes of Wrath*. I finished the unit with a handful of short stories.

Hanging in with challenging students means that we are teaching more than the mandated objectives: we are teaching people. It means we are always attending to the secondary curriculum. That attention to broader student skills and the evolving needs of individual students takes time. The effort to not merely cover the curriculum but to "uncover" it determines a different set of objectives. It determines different lesson plans, different forms of student evaluation, and different forms of teacher evaluation. And I had another concern then: As the class read *The Old Man and the Sea*, Leah was falling apart: smoking more marijuana, sleeping in classes, rarely completing homework, often without any school materials.

Asking for Help Is Hard to Do

We all told her the same thing: if you ask for help, you will pass the course and you will graduate. It was our mantra. We would find a way to support every student if they put in the effort. All paperwork and random staff conversations were dropped when a student asked for help. Teachers spent many lunchtimes and prep periods sitting one to one with students, getting them over the hurdles of fears and gaps in skills. The mantra seemed so simple to us, and yet asking for help for many challenging students is a barrier of massive dimensions. The pluggers came for help. Leah didn't. She was so depressed that she didn't think she deserved our help. Perhaps it would just be another failure, another disappointment.

We continued to give her attention, and continued to praise her effort to drag herself to school. We offered additional resources, such as drug counseling. Breaking her self-destructive habits required persistent kindness, personalized expectations, opportunities to self-reflect, and direct feedback on her condition—the school culture was built to hang in through 100 repetitions of such dialogues to help her make better decisions. Leah's in-school therapist took the lead on talking with her about her addiction. The rest of us reached for as much of Leah's strengths as she had access to each day.

Then her school therapist came to a team meeting with an announcement: Leah had agreed to check herself into a substance abuse facility. In a meeting that included the therapist, Leah, and her mother, Leah finally admitted that she did need help. The therapist's work with Leah had been a vital relationship of support, helping her hang in at school, and now in acknowledging her feelings of desperation. The therapist got on the phone and found a facility with an opening that accepted Leah's mother's insurance. Her mother walked with her to their car, and they drove to the treatment facility. I didn't get to say good-bye. I didn't know if she would return to the school. Many substance abusers can't go back to their former friends and locales because these associations can lead to relapses.

One of the professional hazards and rewards of hanging in with challenging students is that we develop meaningful relationships with them, even within the critical limits of professional boundaries. Leah drew out the best of me as a teacher. I thought each day about how to reel her into a lesson and how to get her to acknowledge her accomplishments. Every lesson plan had her in mind. I was a grizzled enough veteran at this point in my career to know that my own feelings of success could not be in one-to-one correspondence with Leah's successes. I could have a good day as a teacher even if she had a bad day as a student. As a professional, I needed to know that I had done my very best, even if she could not reciprocate.

Saying Good-Bye Well Is Part of the Curriculum

In her seminal work *On Death and Dying*, Elisabeth Kübler-Ross (1969) suggests that we acknowledge in some fashion all the losses we face in our lives as a curriculum that prepares us for the more significant deaths we will ultimately face when those we love pass away. When a pen ran out of ink in my class, I asked the students for a moment of silence before dropping it in the wastebasket. It was a funny ritual. Acknowledging classroom pets that died was part of the curriculum, a ritual that wasn't funny. Leah and her costudents had experienced more deaths of peers in their communities than seemed natural, and acknowledging them had to be part of our work. Many challenging students have had far too many people in their lives precipitously disappear; those unplanned disappearances left scars.

There were a handful of ways in which the school took care of students who had suffered a traumatic loss. Often students needed time out of class to sit with a therapist. Sometimes they just needed to know that their teachers were aware of their loss, but were not going to say anything about it. Sometimes it was important that each staff person take a gentle moment to acknowledge that we had heard of their loss. The therapists communicated to the teaching team what was planned for each student. When the loss was experienced by the entire community, we set aside time for groups of students who wanted to talk about it—and just as importantly, planned a simultaneous typical class period for those students who felt that they could cope best by sticking to their routines and getting work done. Loss has both personal and collective elements. I felt the loss of Leah and was consoled that she finally had asked for help and was getting it.

I also wasn't sure we had done enough to help her. This is another professional hazard. As was the case with Jasmine (Chapter 9), there are always more interventions to try and more combinations of various interventions. The school had practiced "harm reduction" with Leah, working with her to understand and reduce her substance use; she had a solid working relationship with her therapist, had been willing to try reducing her use, kept up her attendance, and was not abusing substances such as heroin that could literally kill her overnight. Many other programs subscribe to a zero-tolerance practice, in which any substance use by a student prompts decisions about expulsion. Perhaps we hadn't pushed hard enough for her to get treatment. Perhaps I had let my focus on her potential undermine a stricter set of academic expectations. Had I protected her too much from the lessons she could have learned from failing (Benson, 2012)?

As a small community filled with challenges, our school regularly faced the sudden departure of a student. Some, such as Leah, needed hospitalizations. Some dropped out. Some were withdrawn by their families or the towns that had funded them. Some needed to go to a school that was better resourced to meet their particular needs. We developed a ritual to acknowledge these changes, knowing that we also had to respect the privacy and confidentiality of the students. Their business was not everyone's business, but they all held a place in the community. At our weekly all-school meeting, the agenda included a time called "transitions," when the comings and goings of staff and students would be announced: "John has decided to return to public school." "Joaquin is coming back on Tuesday." "Amber is finishing her internship next week." "Leah is taking a break from school to get additional treatment."

Through Leah's dedicated single mother, the school therapist kept track of Leah's progress and consistently conveyed the message that we would welcome Leah back when she completed her treatment. Weeks passed. Leah had had a setback. Her discharge date was rescheduled. Then we heard she was taking classes at the treatment facility. She had earned new privileges. She had a job. Then one day, months after she had asked for help, her therapist said Leah was set to return. We found places for her in our classes. Of course, I advocated for her to be in my class.

"Her mom said that Leah asked not to be back in your class," I was told.

"What? No, really? Why?" I wanted to finish the work. I wanted her to see how happy I was that she was coming back. And in that moment, I knew that I had experienced some very deep countertransference. I wanted to be the special one for her. She had no dad; there were ways that Leah reminded me of my own daughter. I had never said a word to her about that. I had never told my students that I had a daughter their age. I didn't want them to think I would be comparing them to her. I had also learned that we shouldn't think of ourselves as "the better parent," better than the students' own parents. We were with the students for a very small section of the arc of their lives; their families were in it for the long haul. It is funny and telling in schools when a student accidentally calls a teacher "Mom." It is more problematic when we think of ourselves that way.

"Leah says that you think she is a screw-up. She's disappointed you. She says she respects you immensely as a teacher, but maybe she'll do better with someone else." What had I done wrong to prompt this rejection? Oh, right, this wasn't about me. What mattered was that Leah was ready to return.

She did return, and she did great when she came back. She was a plugger. She went to recovery meetings every evening after school. She asked for help and stayed with the work until she was successful. She kept her socializing with peers to a bare minimum. She dressed neatly, kept her book bag organized, and displayed a determination that seemed to preclude spontaneity. When I saw her in passing, I would say, "I hear you are doing great. I am happy for you." She would smile briefly and move on.

At graduation, her mother gave me a warm hug. "When she came back, she told me she was going to prove you were wrong about her," her mom said. I must have opened my mouth to protest, because she quickly added, "Don't worry about it. She needed someone to measure herself against, and look how well she did."

The Teacher Says Good-Bye

The last best lesson we give students is how we leave them. After 20 years, it was my time to leave the school. Inevitably, the day came when at our community meeting during transitions time I announced that I was leaving. Our ritual was to give the students three to four weeks' notice. That could be enough time for students to cycle through the stages of grieving that Kübler-Ross (1969) defined:

- *Denial*—"You're not really leaving, right?"

- *Anger*—"Go ahead and leave."
- *Bargaining*—"What if everyone got together and told you they wanted you to stay?"
- *Depression*—"Nothing is going to be the same around here after you go. It's going to be terrible."
- *Acceptance*—"Thanks for helping me. I'll miss you. Good luck."

Students need time to experience those stages, but not so long that saying good-bye interferes with attention to other matters.

I had seen many staff come and go, as had the students, but it was a different experience being that person. I was terminating scores of relationships. Following the advice of a mentor of mine, I wrote each student an individual note. Each note mentioned something very specific the student had done that had mattered to me in my work and how their efforts inspired mine, because, even for our most challenging students, there was truth in our work together. Their gift to me (and I think this came from the prompting of a teacher) was that they wrote back to me the same type of notes. We said our good-byes well.

Hanging-In Recommendations and Considerations for Individual Students

1. *Understand the variety of cultural norms involving death and loss that specifically affect the life of a given student.* There are expectations of when, how, and if you should talk to students about traumatic losses in their lives, depending on their family and community.
2. *Support students who may not be able to explicitly ask for help.* For some, the phrase "Do you need help?" or even the word "help" reinforces their sense of inadequacy. Ask the question in a variety of ways: "I might have an idea here for you. Would you be interested in hearing it?" "I've seen some other students struggle with this. I can pass along what they did to get going."

3. *Develop an unobtrusive, special signal for when a help-avoidant student needs help:* a hand on her head, a book upright on the desk, two quick fingers in the air. The privacy of the request in the public space of the classroom can allow some challenging students to get what they need.

4. *Tell students you intend for them to work as hard as they can on this day.* By saying this, you communicate a belief in their potential and an understanding that they come to school with burdens.

5. *Reflect on a student's behavior, not your hypothesis that they may be under the influence.* It is hard to know if students are under the influence of a drug. Perhaps they did not get any sleep, or they ran out of their prescription medication. Say, "Leah, you are having trouble keeping your head up today, and your eyes are very red. You are not doing your best work." Then make a timely report to the school nurse. Describing behavior is especially critical in the absence of a team plan to address a particular student's addiction concerns.

6. *Make sure you find one-to-one time for a brief good-bye.* Your attention to this transition can impact how a student summarizes your entire working relationship. Articulate the mutual lessons learned.

Hanging-In Recommendations and Considerations for the Adult Team

1. *Storytelling:* Share what rituals you have used to say good-bye to students. How have you helped students move on when a peer or staff member has left the school?

2. *Never speak poorly in any public setting about a student,* not even after the student has left your school. Teachers can discuss their frustrations with each other one to one, but not in large groups. The emphasis on exquisite respectfulness is not suspended when a student has stopped attending.

3. *Review the elements of the school environment (procedures, rituals, objects) that communicate your mission.* Brainstorm ways to maximize that influence on a day-to-day basis. Teachers can bring these ideas into their own classrooms.

4. *Develop specific plans, and scripts for staff, to address a student's substance use.* Some students need persistent staff reflections on their behaviors (see recommendation 5 in the list for individual students). Others need direct feedback: "Leah, your behavior is the behavior of someone who is under the influence."

5. *Review what happened when a student has left the program.* Teams need to express their feelings and together organize their ideas into a shared learning experience: "What was our best hope for Leah? What did we do? What did Leah learn from our work? What could we have done more of, or differently?"

Hanging-In Recommendations and Considerations for Administrators

1. *Make explicit the procedures, structures, and rituals of the school that the administration prioritizes.* Administrative actions *and* words combine to support a school culture. Invest in building the school culture, which is reflected in high test scores but is not measured solely in those scores.

2. *Develop a school team to deal with issues of substance abuse.* This team will define procedures, provide training, and maintain records of interventions. It is important that classroom staff not be expected to improvise their responses.

3. *Develop a school team to deal with tragic losses in the school community.*

4. *Develop schoolwide rituals for saying good-byes.* Many challenging students have experienced more traumatic transitions than their peers. School can be where they feel nurtured at times of loss and learn how to say good-bye well.

References

Armstrong, T. (2012, October). First discover their strengths. *Educational Leadership, 70*(2), 10–16.

Atwool, N. (2006). Attachment and resilience: Implications for children in care. *Child Care in Practice, 12*(4), 315–330.

Bailey, B., Christian, H., Hepler, V., & Speidel, A. (2011). *Creating the school family: Bully-proofing classrooms through emotional intelligence.* Oviedo, FL: Loving Guidance.

Beck, M. (2012, October 29). Inside the mind of perfectionists. *Wall Street Journal.* Retrieved from http://online.wsj.com/article/SB10001424052970204840504578085802751238578.html

Benson, J. (2012, October). 100 repetitions. *Educational Leadership, 70*(2), 76–78.

Brookhart, S. M. (2008). *How to give effective feedback to your students.* Alexandria, VA: ASCD.

Brooks, J. G., & Brooks, M. G. (1993). *In search of understanding: The case for constructivist classrooms.* Alexandria, VA: ASCD.

Brown, L. S. (2004, January). Feminist paradigms of trauma treatment. *Psychotherapy: Theory, Research, Practice, Training, 41*(4), 464–471.

Brualdi Timmins, A. C. (1998). Classroom questions. *Practical Assessment, Research & Evaluation, 6*(6). Retrieved from http://pareonline.net/getvn.asp?v=6&n=6

Canada, G. (1995). *Fist, stick, knife, gun: A personal history of violence in America.* Boston: Beacon Press.

Cleveland, K. P. (2011). *Teaching boys who struggle in school: Strategies that turn underachievers into successful learners.* Alexandria, VA: ASCD.

Cole, S. F., O'Brien, J. G., Gadd, M. G., Ristuccia, J., Wallace, D. L., & Gregory, M. (2005). *Helping traumatized children learn: Supportive school environments for children traumatized by family violence.* Boston: Massachusetts Advocates for Children.

Dewey, J. (1916/2004). *Democracy and education.* Mineola, NY: Dover Publications.

Dewey, J. (1938). *Experience and education.* New York: Macmillan.

Elbow, P. (1986). *Embracing contraries: Explorations in learning and teaching.* New York: Oxford University Press.

Fisher, R., Ury, W., & Patton, B. (1991). *Getting to yes: Negotiating agreement without giving in* (2nd ed.). New York: Penguin Books.

Greene, R. W. (1998). *The explosive child: A new approach for understanding and parenting easily frustrated, chronically inflexible children.* New York: HarperCollins.

Hallowell, E. (June 24, 2012). ADHD is not your fault [blog post]. Retrieved from http://www.drhallowell.com/blog/adhd-is-not-your-fault/

Hartley, S. L., Barker, E. T., Seltzer, M. M., Floyd, F., Greenberg, J., Orsmond, G., & Bolt, D. (2010, August). The relative risk and timing of divorce in families of children with an autism spectrum disorder. *Journal of Family Psychology, 24*(4), 449–457.

Hattie, J. A. (2009). *Visible learning: A synthesis of over 800 meta-analyses relating to achievement.* London: Routledge.

Hawkins, D. B. (n.d.). Quote retrieved from http://www.goodreads.com/quotes/80238-all-of-us-must-cross-the-line-between-ignorance-and

Hoerr, T. R. (2005). *The art of school leadership.* Alexandria, VA: ASCD.

Holt, J. C. (1964). *How children fail.* New York: Pitman.

Kübler-Ross, E. (1969). *On death and dying.* New York: Macmillan.

Medina, J. (2008). *Brain rules: 12 principles for surviving and thriving at work, home, and school.* Seattle, WA: Pear Press.

Meier, D. (1995). *The power of their ideas: Lessons for America from a small school in Harlem.* Boston: Beacon Press.

Mendler, A. (2012). *When teaching gets tough.* Alexandria, VA: ASCD.

Metz, M. H. (1993). Teachers' ultimate dependence on their students. In J. W. Little & M. W. McLaughlin (Eds.), *Teachers' work: Individuals, colleagues, and contexts* (pp. 104–136). New York: Teachers College Press.

Miller, J. B., Jordan, J. V., Kaplan, A. G., Stiver, I. P., & Surrey, J. L. (1997). Some misconceptions and reconceptions of a relational approach. In J. V. Jordan (Ed.), *Women's growth in diversity: More writings from the Stone Center* (pp. 25–49). New York: Guilford Press.

Nakkula, M. J., & Toshalis, E. (2006). *Understanding youth: Adolescent development for educators.* Cambridge, MA: Harvard Education Press.

National Center for Higher Education Management Systems. (2013). Preparation for college: Public high school graduation rates. Retrieved from http://www.higheredinfo.org/dbrowser/index.php?submeasure=36&year=2009&level=nation&mode=graph&state=0

Ogden, P., & Minton, K. (2000, October). Sensorimotor psychotherapy: One method for processing traumatic memory. *Traumatology, 6*(3). Retrieved from http://www.sensorimotorpsychotherapy.org/articles.html

Rogers, C. R. (1961). *On becoming a person.* Boston: Houghton Mifflin.

Saphier, J., & Gower, R. R. (1997). *The skillful teacher: Building your teaching skills* (5th ed.). Acton, MA: Research for Better Teaching.

Siegel, D. J. (1999). *The developing mind: How relationships and the brain interact to shape who we are.* New York: Guilford Press.

Tatum, A. W. (2005). *Teaching reading to black adolescent males: Closing the achievement gap.* Portland, ME: Stenhouse.

Taylor, J. F. (2001). *From defiance to cooperation: Real solutions for transforming the angry, defiant, discouraged child.* Roseville, CA: Prima Pub.

Tomlinson, C. A. (2012, October). One to grow on: Rising to the challenge of challenging behavior. *Educational Leadership, 70*(2), 88–89.

Truss, L. (2004). *Eats, shoots & leaves: The zero tolerance approach to punctuation.* New York: Gotham Books.

Ungar, M. (2008). Putting resilience theory in action: Five principles for intervention. In L. Liebenberg & M. Ungar (Eds.), *Resilience in action: Working with youth across cultures and contexts* (pp. 17–37). Toronto: University of Toronto Press.

U.S. Census Bureau. (2008). Table 2a Employment size of employer and non-employer firms, 2008. Retrieved from http://www.census.gov/econ/smallbus .html

Vail, P. L. (1994). *Emotion: The on/off switch for learning.* Rosemont, NJ: Modern Learning Press.

Wegman, L., & O'Banion, A. M. (2013). Students affected by physical and emotional abuse. In E. A. Rossen & R. Hull (Eds.), *Supporting and educating traumatized students: A guide for school-based professionals* (pp. 219–228). Oxford: Oxford University Press.

Index

■ ■ ■

About the Author

Jeffrey Benson has worked in almost every school context in his 35 years of experience in education: as a teacher in elementary, middle, and high schools; as an instructor in undergraduate and graduate programs; and as an administrator in day and residential schools. He has studied and worked side by side with national leaders in the fields of special education, learning theory, trauma and addiction, school reform, adult development, and conflict resolution. He has been a consultant to public and private schools, mentored teachers and principals in varied school settings, and has written on many school-based issues. The core of Jeffrey Benson's work is in understanding how people learn—the starting point for everything that schools should do. He can be reached via e-mail at JeffreyBenson@LeadersAndLearners.org; his Twitter handle is @JeffreyBenson61.

Related ASCD Resources: Helping Students with Challenges to Learn

At the time of publication, the following ASCD resources were available (ASCD stock numbers appear in parentheses). For up-to-date information about ASCD resources, go to www.ascd.org. You can search the complete archives of *Educational Leadership* at http://www.ascd.org/el.

Professional Interest Communities

Visit the ASCD website and scroll to the bottom to click on "professional interest communities." Within these communities, find information about professional educators who have formed groups around topics like "Affective Factors in Learning" and "Multiple Intelligences."

ASCD Edge™ Groups

Exchange ideas and connect with other educators interested in various topics, including Intervention and Remediation, on the social networking site ASCD EDge™.

Online Courses

Bullying: Taking Charge, 2nd Edition (#PD11OC105)

Classroom Management: Building Effective Relationships, 2nd Edition (#PD11OC104)

Conflict Resolution: An Introduction (#PD09OC21)

Response to Intervention: An Introduction (#PD11OC100)

Print Products

Classroom Strategies for Helping At-Risk Students by David R. Snow (#105106)

Connecting with Students by Allen Mendler (#101236)

Discipline with Diginity, 3rd Edition: New Challenges, New Solutions by Allen Mendler, Richard Curwin, and Brian Mendler (#108036)

Getting to Got It: Helping Struggling Students Learn How to Learn by Betty K. Garner (#107024)

Managing Your Classroom with Heart: A Guide for Nurturing Adolescent Learners by Katy Ridnouer (#107013)

Meeting Students Where They Live: Motivation in Urban Schools by Richard Curwin (#109110)

The Motivated Student: Unlocking the Enthusiasm for Learning by Bob Sullo (#109028)

The Respectful School: How Educators and Students Can Conquer Hate and Harrassment by William Preble and Stephen Wessler (#103006)

The Whole Child Initiative

The Whole Child Initiative helps schools and communities create learning environments that allow students to be healthy, safe, engaged, supported, and challenged. To learn more about other books and resources that relate to the whole child, visit www.wholechildeducation.org.

For more information: send e-mail to member@ascd.org; call 1-800-933-2723 or 703-578-9600, press 2; send a fax to 703-575-5400; or write to Information Services, ASCD, 1703 N. Beauregard St., Alexandria, VA 22311-1714 USA.